Steck Vaughn

Target Spelling 1260

Teacher's Edition

Margaret Scarborough
Mary F. Brigham
Teresa A. Miller

Meet your state standards with free blackline masters and links to other materials at www.HarcourtAchieve.com/AchievementZone.
Click Steck-Vaughn Standards.

Acknowledgment
Cover Illustration by Dan Clayton

ISBN 0-7398-9199-5
© 2004 Harcourt Achieve Inc.

Harcourt Achieve
Rigby • Steck-Vaughn

www.HarcourtAchieve.com
1.800.531.5015

Contents

About the Authors

Margaret M. Scarborough teaches at Elizabeth Seawell Elementary School in Chapel Hill, North Carolina. Her master's degree was conferred by the University of North Carolina. Ms. Scarborough has taught kindergarten through sixth-grade students with special learning needs. She works collaboratively with regular classroom teachers, remedial reading teachers, speech and language pathologists, and behavioral therapists. She is a member of the Learning Disabilities Association of North Carolina and past president of the Orange County Association for Children and Adults with Learning Disabilities.

Mary F. Brigham is the principal of Bowley Elementary School in Fort Bragg, North Carolina. She has been a principal for ten years—four years at McNair Elementary School and six years at Bowley Elementary School. Ms. Brigham has led language arts, early childhood, and remedial reading programs for the Fort Bragg Schools, in addition to having had varied teaching experience at all levels. Ms. Brigham earned her master's degree at the University of North Carolina at Chapel Hill and completed a doctorate in Educational Administration in 1992 at Campbell University.

Teresa A. Miller has taught children in Virginia, Vermont, and North Carolina. Her degrees in education are from the College of William and Mary and the University of North Carolina at Chapel Hill. She works with both children and adults in a wide variety of educational settings.

Target Spelling is an alternative spelling program for students with special learning needs. The program was created by specialists in learning disabilities and remedial reading at Elizabeth Seawell Elementary School in Chapel Hill, North Carolina. The authors successfully used the program with their students before its publication. *Target Spelling* has since become a tried-and-true favorite of teachers. *Target Spelling* provides teachers with an excellent tool to use in guiding students in the strategies that good spellers use and in providing students with opportunities for practice.

This edition of *Target Spelling* retains the spelling strategies and features of the

original program that have repeatedly led students to spelling success, while adding several new features requested by teachers. Now with more opportunities for writing experiences, additional opportunities for review, even more focus on spelling strategies, a Word Study Plan, and standardized test practice pages, *Target Spelling* will maximize student learning.

> *"Spelling is a complex language system with phonetic, semantic, historical, and visual demands."*
> (Gentry & Gillet, *Teaching Kids to Spell*)

Each of the first three books—*Target 180, 360,* and *540*—present 180 words. The next three books—*Target 780, 1020,* and *1260*—each contain 240 words. The book titles are derived from the number of spelling words students have mastered as they complete each book successively.

To meet the needs of students with special needs, *Target Spelling* incorporates these features:

- A placement test to determine the proper entry level for each student
- A systematic method of study that provides a variety of stimulating and meaningful exercises—appropriate to a wide range of ages and abilities—to reinforce a positive attitude toward the study of spelling
- A limited number of spelling words introduced each week—six per week in *Target 180, 360,* and *540;* eight per week in *Target 780, 1020,* and *1260*
- A master word list for teachers to use in coordinating spelling instruction with the total language arts curriculum
- Instructional activities to accommodate a variety of learning modalities
- Relaxed pacing from lesson to lesson
- Clear, concise directions for each exercise
- Cloze paragraphs to test students' ability to use the spelling words in context
- Additional review pages every five lessons to reinforce student learning
- A checklist and a graph on which students can track their progress
- Standardized test practice pages to allow students to gain familiarity and comfort with test formats

Target Spelling is comprised of six worktexts based on the concept that the learning of spelling is a means to an end—to help students become better communicators—and not an end in itself. The aim of the program is to lead students to discover underlying linguistic patterns and relationships so that they can apply what they learn in *Target Spelling* to their other reading and writing experiences.

The lessons in *Target Spelling* follow a carefully designed instructional plan. The focus is on patterns and strategies, instead of spelling rules, to make the challenges of written communication easier for students with special needs. Words from a word family, such as "Words with -*ack*," are presented along with high-utility sight words to give students the quickest access to spelling the words they speak.

The first three books of *Target Spelling*—*180, 360,* and *540*—contain 162 of the 220 words from the Dolch Basic Sight Word List. The words on this list are "high frequency" words, or words that occur often in written and spoken language. The words in the next three books—*780, 1020,* and *1260*—include words with more complex linguistic patterns, commonly misspelled homonyms, phonemic patterns with prefixes and suffixes, and words of up to four syllables.

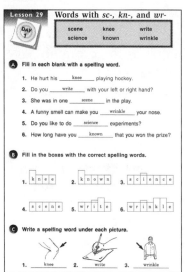

Each *Target Spelling* book is organized into thirty weeks of lessons, with four exercise pages per lesson. Lesson and day numbers are clearly indicated, and student pages are perforated to facilitate use. One exercise page is to be used each day for the first four days of the week (Days 1–4).

On the last day of the week (Day 5), teachers can administer the spelling test, using the dictation sentences provided on pages T13–T15. Students can write the spelling words on their own notebook paper.

My Word List at the back of each student book provides a place for students to record their weekly test results and to practice missed spelling words. A progress graph for recording weekly test scores is also provided. Review pages in the Pupil Edition and blackline master Review pages in the Teacher's Edition are available after every five lessons and can be used as alternate assessment tools or extra practice for students who need it. In addition, standardized test practice is available to help familiarize students with test formats.

New to this edition are features in the student book designed to provide more support for students with special needs.

- The *Word Study Plan* demonstrates a step-by-step method for learning to spell words.

- The *Spelling Strategies* page describes simple techniques that all good spellers use.

- *Review* pages after every five lessons help students review and maintain strategies, skills, and spelling patterns.

- The *Word Study Sheet* provides a framework for students as they read, spell, and write new words.

- *Graph Your Progress* encourages students to take ownership of their learning as they plot their spelling mastery from week to week.

"Children need to learn how to spell, not what to spell. They need generalizable strategies that can be applied in all spelling contexts."
(Rosencrans, *The Spelling Book*)

Target Spelling can be used flexibly to help meet the needs of students with spelling problems. The exercises are designed to be completed independently by students after each task has been introduced and explained by the teacher.

To facilitate learning and to allow students with special needs to implement spelling strategies, *Target Spelling* provides the following types of exercises:

- **Writing Practice** Many opportunities are provided for students to recognize and use spelling words in context. Prompts encourage students to write original sentences and, in the higher-level *Target Spelling* books, original paragraphs.

- **Cloze Paragraphs** This widely endorsed learning technique enables students to develop a broad range of vocabulary and reading skills.

- **Word Analysis** Students focus on elements of a word, examining similarities and differences among features of the spelling words. In this manner, students make their own generalizations about correct spelling.

- **Definition/Clue Exercises** Common meanings are reinforced and new meanings are taught. Students practice writing the spelling words.

- **Crossword Puzzles** This entertaining format guides students to understand the components of a word, its meaning, and its relationship to other words.

- **Review** To help students maintain and review strategies and skills, review pages are provided after every five lessons. The familiar formats of the pages foster student success.

- **Standardized Test Practice** To acquaint students with test formats, exercises are presented in formats students will encounter on standardized tests.

To further assist teachers, the following features are also included:

Placement Test This test helps teachers target words that students are unable to spell correctly. Teachers can test students before assigning specific *Target Spelling* books to them.

Dictation Sentences Sentences that use spelling words in context are provided to further enhance students' ability to understand and spell words in context. These sentences may be used when the weekly test is administered or as a reinforcement exercise. Spelling words from earlier *Target Spelling* lessons are often included to help students connect to previous learning.

Blackline Masters A variety of blackline masters are designed to be used flexibly to help teachers meet student learning needs. The *Word Study Sheet* describes the seven-step plan for student use in independent word study, and two assessment tools assist with record-keeping and documentation. The *Checklist for Informal Assessment* can be used to observe students' progress, and the *Student Progress Graph* may be used to graph the number of words a student spells correctly on his or her weekly test. In addition, review practice reinforces the content of the previous five lessons.

> *"Good spellers use different strategies to try words."*
> (Snowball & Bolton, *Spelling K–8*)

Meet your state standards with free blackline masters and links to other materials at **www.HarcourtAchieve.com/AchievementZone**. Click **Steck-Vaughn Standards**.

Determine Which Book to Use

Several tools can be used to determine which book is most appropriate for students. Teachers can consider students' approximate reading level, as well as use writing samples to evaluate spelling errors. The *Placement Test*, described on page T11, is designed to accurately gauge which *Target Spelling* book will be the most appropriate learning tool.

Introduce the Weekly Lesson

If using *Target 180*, teachers should read each word aloud and use it in a sentence. In other *Target Spelling* books, students can be involved in presenting the words. After the words are read aloud, guide students in a discussion about the words' meanings and about their relationship to one another.

Use the Exercises

A variety of exercises that utilize a multisensory approach involve students in learning and practicing the spelling words. As students first begin the exercises, teachers can explain and model the directions for the pages. (See pages T7 and T8 for more specific examples of exercise formats.) As students become more familiar with the types of exercises, less modeling will be needed. When students understand the task, they can complete the pages independently. Then teachers can vary the method of evaluating the exercises. An answer key is provided for teachers to use when checking each exercise. Teachers may wish to involve students in checking their work as a group activity, or provide the answer key for students to use in self-checking.

Assess Student Learning

The *Dictation Sentences*, beginning on page T13, can be used to measure student mastery. Mastery occurs when students miss no more than two spelling words. If students do not attain mastery, teachers can review and reteach. Encourage students to use *My Word List* to practice missed words. Teachers may also wish to use the dictation sentences as a pretest to help assess student needs.

Additional opportunities for assessment are presented in the student books as well as in the blackline masters in the Teacher's Edition:

- *Review* pages in both the Teacher's Edition and Pupil Edition can be used to check how well students are retaining mastery of five lessons.

- Standardized test format pages allow students to practice test-taking strategies while demonstrating mastery.

- *Graph Your Progress* presents an easy-to-use format for students to track their progress.

- The *Checklist for Informal Assessment* and the *Student Progress Graph* provide formats for observing and documenting skill growth.

"Assessment should be comprehensive and eclectic."
(Rosencrans, *The Spelling Book*)

The Exercises

The range of exercises in *Target Spelling* provides teachers with the opportunity to discover which approaches are most successful with individual students. The following exercises appear frequently in *Target Spelling* books. Their complexity and level of challenge increase as students move through the program. Throughout the exercises, students are given opportunities to practice and apply spelling strategies.

Recognition in Context

These activities reinforce learning of a word's meaning by requiring students to recognize the spelling word in context, or to supply the missing word in context.

A. Circle the spelling word. Then write it on the line.

1. (Can) you come to see me? _can_

B. Fill in each blank with the correct spelling word.

1. May I have _an_ apple?
   at an

C. Fill in each blank with a spelling word.

1. You are my _best_ friend.

Cloze paragraphs are also frequently provided. Cloze paragraphs sharpen students' comprehension and strengthen their spelling skills. Teachers should direct students to read or listen to the entire passage before selecting the missing words. If students don't immediately recognize the appropriate word, suggest that they try each spelling word in the blank and reason through the choices. To modify this activity for auditory learners, record and play each cloze paragraph for students to use as they work the exercise.

Visual Discrimination

In these activities, students must be able to discriminate spelling words among words with similar letters. This format focuses students' attention on spelling patterns.

A. Circle the word that is the same as the top one.

rag	find	bag
raq	tind	bay
rab	fiud	dag
(rag)	(find)	beg
rap	finb	(bag)

B. Find the hidden spelling words.

```
e   l   e  (t   e   s   t)
s   o  (b   u   n   g   s
a   r   e   b   e   s   t)
s   e  (w   e   s   t)  u
t   r   o   n   t   s   r
```

C. Put an *X* on the word that is **not the same.**

1. draw   draw   draw   ~~darw~~   draw
2. plow   plow   plow   ~~glow~~   plow
3. clown   clown   ~~clawn~~   clown   clown
4. frown   frown   frown   frown   ~~frowm~~

D. Circle each spelling word that is hidden in the big word. Write the word on the line.

1. (wag)on   _wag_   2. b(rag)   _rag_

Word Analysis

These activities require students to examine all facets of the spelling words, such as individual letters and word families so that they focus on elements of the words, as well as the word as a whole unit.

A. Find the missing letters. Then write the word.

1. p l a i n   plain
2. t r a i l   trail

B. Fill in the boxes with the correct spelling word.

1. rag   2. find   3. bag

C. Circle the letters that are the same in each spelling word.

peach   heat   clean   beans   read

D. Write the spelling word that rhymes with the word pair.

1. sing   thing   swing
2. pair   fair   hair

E. Write words that begin like each spelling word below.

whale   flake   snake
what   fly   snow

Crossword puzzles are another word analysis format used in *Target Spelling*.

Writing Practice

Students are directed to write spelling words accurately two or three times as a kinesthetic approach to learning the spelling words. The format of the exercise is designed to have students write the spelling words, rather than circling or underlining responses, to maximize the learning opportunities.

Creative Writing

Students apply what they have learned about spelling patterns and strategies in writing. Students may be asked to complete sentences, or write original sentences, using spelling words. In higher levels of *Target Spelling,* students are directed to write paragraphs.

A. Complete each sentence.

1. It's <u>her</u> turn to _____.
2. The <u>fern</u> I bought is _____.

Matching Words with Pictures

In these exercises, students practice recognizing visual cues and matching print to pictures by labeling illustrations with the correct spelling word.

Definition/Clue Exercises

These exercises reinforce meanings of spelling words in an entertaining and challenging way. Students draw conclusions to solve riddles or make associations, such as antonyms or synonyms.

A. Answer each question with a spelling word.

1. Which word is the same as two nickels?
   dime

2. Which word names a part of the body?
   spine

B. Write each spelling word beside its clue.

sea   1. the ocean
pail   2. a bucket

C. Write the spelling word that names things you can touch.

1. foot   2. book   3. wood

Throughout *Target Spelling*, students are encouraged to use spelling strategies to correctly spell words. Spelling strategies can help students notice word families and patterns among words, examine words visually to build a sense of what "looks right" in spelling, and think about the sounds of the words they are trying to spell. Spelling strategies create links between what students already know and new concepts.

• Strategies are described in easy-to-follow language on the *Spelling Strategies* page in the Pupil Edition. Simple tips that students can return to again and again are introduced.

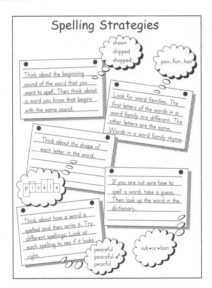

• The *Word Study Plan* in the Pupil Edition applies the strategies, giving students suggestions for things to try when spelling words.

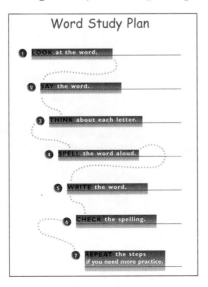

• The *Word Study Sheet* in the Pupil Edition guides students to apply the strategies as they work to spell the words. A blackline master of the *Word Study Sheet* is also provided in the Teacher's Edition.

Word Study Sheet							
Words	1 Look at the Word	2 Say the Word	3 Think About Each Letter	4 Spell the Word Aloud	5 Write the Word	6 Check the Spelling	7 Repeat Steps (if needed)

Name _____

Guiding with Questions

Teachers can help students self-monitor and rely on strategies by prompting them with questions such as the following:

• What other word does this remind you of?

• Does it look right?

• What letters can stand for that sound?

• Close your eyes. Can you see the word?

• Is there a word part that you know?

• Do you recognize any word families?

• Can you find the word in the dictionary?

"Competent spellers use many strategies to try unfamiliar words and to learn words."
(Snowball & Bolton, *Spelling K–8*)

Activities for Various Learning Modalities

The authors of *Target Spelling* recognize that students learn in different ways. The program addresses three different learning styles: visual, auditory, and kinesthetic. Teachers can enhance student learning by presenting the following activities geared toward certain learning modalities.

Visual Learners

Write a short word, such as *an* on the board. One at a time, students add a letter to make a new word.

Have students change one letter of a spelling word to make new words.

Write spelling words on the board. Direct students to find smaller words within the word.

Have students illustrate spelling words and label the illustrations.

Draw a tic-tac-toe or crossword pattern and direct students to fill in words.

Write spelling words in one column on the board. Write words with a similar pattern in another column. Have students match words with close spellings.

Write any mnemonic devices, such as "The principal is your pal."

Kinesthetic Learners

Give each student in a small group one letter card of a spelling word. Have students arrange themselves in order to spell the word.

Label bags or boxes with word patterns. Give students word cards to sort according to pattern.

Write spelling words on the board. Have students use colored chalk to mark a spelling pattern in each word.

Have students type the spelling words or related words on a typewriter or computer keyboard.

Have teams of students act out the meaning of spelling words in a game of "Charades."

Have students trace spelling words cut from sandpaper letters.

Auditory Learners

Have students say and spell each word into a tape recorder, then play back the tape.

Write words on the board, circling a vowel, consonant, or pattern. Ask students to pronounce the sound the circled letters stand for, then name other words with that sound.

Recite a rhyme, short story, or series of sentences. Ask students to clap or make another signal when they hear spelling words.

Make letter cards with target sounds and word cards of the spelling words. Distribute the word cards to students. Hold up a sound card and have students hold up corresponding word cards and spell the word in unison.

The Placement Test

The Placement Test helps teachers target words that students are unable to spell correctly. Then students can be assigned an appropriate level of exercises.

Students should be tested individually, and only on the words within their instructional reading level. Teachers should call out the first word in a level, use the word in a sentence, and then repeat the word. It is recommended that when students miss three or more words at any level, this becomes the level at which they should be placed. The circled numbers to the left of each word group indicate instructional reading levels.

The following chart will aid teachers in placing students:

WORDS ON PLACEMENT TEST	NUMBER OF WORDS MISSED	BOOK INDICATED
1–10	Three or more	Target 180
11–20	Three or more	Target 360
21–30	Three or more	Target 540
31–40	Three or more	Target 780
41–50	Three or more	Target 1020
51–60	Three or more	Target 1260

1

TARGET 180

1.	can	I can run very fast.	can
2.	pen	Please help me put the pig in the pen.	pen
3.	rack	I hung my coat on the rack.	rack
4.	hill	Let's walk up that steep hill.	hill
5.	pond	The ducks swim in the pond.	pond
6.	nest	The birds built a nest in the tree.	nest
7.	silk	Her new dress was made of silk.	silk
8.	mitten	He lost one mitten while playing outside.	mitten
9.	are	You are a good friend.	are
10.	have	Have you been to see the circus?	have

2

TARGET 360

11.	hurt	I fell down and hurt my knee.	hurt
12.	what	What do you want to do today?	what
13.	block	Have you ever seen a block of ice?	block
14.	think	Do you think you can go?	think
15.	trunk	An elephant has a trunk.	trunk
16.	branch	The branch of the tree broke off.	branch
17.	crash	Did you hear about the plane crash?	crash
18.	shift	Do you have to shift gears in your car?	shift
19.	spend	I can spend money very fast.	spend
20.	strung	I strung the tree with lights.	strung

3

TARGET 540

21.	location	Our house has a pretty location.	location
22.	state	What state do you live in?	state
23.	chair	Please sit in that chair.	chair
24.	judge	Who was the judge in the court?	judge
25.	spoil	If you leave the milk out, it will spoil.	spoil
26.	bright	The sun is bright.	bright
27.	frown	When I am sad, I have a frown on my face.	frown
28.	wrinkle	Can you press the wrinkle out of my slacks?	wrinkle
29.	caught	She caught the ball in her glove.	caught
30.	toast	Toast and jelly taste good.	toast

4

TARGET 780

31.	search	We will help you search for your lost dog.	search
32.	launch	They will launch a rocket today.	launch
33.	knew	He knew it was time to go home.	knew
34.	thieves	The thieves were caught yesterday.	thieves
35.	weren't	We weren't able to go skating.	weren't
36.	wrench	She needed a wrench to fix her bike.	wrench
37.	heal	Most cuts heal quickly.	heal
38.	scratches	Our cat scratches those who tickle her.	scratches
39.	freighter	The freighter sailed from New York to France.	freighter
40.	illnesses	He has had both of those illnesses.	illnesses

5

TARGET 1020

41.	hoping	She was hoping it would snow today.	hoping
42.	slammed	The door slammed shut.	slammed
43.	heard	I heard a strange noise.	heard
44.	struggle	Did the animal struggle to get free?	struggle
45.	alphabet	The alphabet contains 26 letters.	alphabet
46.	scene	She painted a lovely scene of the ocean.	scene
47.	continue	He plans to continue the guitar lessons.	continue
48.	jewel	The jewel sparkles in the sun.	jewel
49.	personal	He had something personal to tell me.	personal
50.	vehicle	The vehicle we use most often is the truck.	vehicle

6

TARGET 1260

51.	thoughtful	My friend is thoughtful of others.	thoughtful
52.	you're	I hope you're planning to go with us.	you're
53.	uncertain	I am uncertain about this answer.	uncertain
54.	misfortune	He had the misfortune to lose his wallet.	misfortune
55.	collision	The collision of the cars occurred today.	collision
56.	believable	That story is not believable.	believable
57.	disconnect	Did he disconnect the telephone?	disconnect
58.	principal	The principal of our school is kind.	principal
59.	experience	She had a great camping experience last summer.	experience
60.	encouragement	With your encouragement, I will win the race.	encouragement

The following are sample placement test results that indicate placement for *Target 180, 360,* and *540.* The placement tests for *Target 780, 1020,* and *1260* should generally begin with word number 31.

This result indicates placement in *Target 180.*

1. can
2. pen
~~3.~~ reck (rack)
4. hill
~~5.~~ pant (pond)
~~6.~~ mess (nest)
~~7.~~ mik (silk)

STOP TEST

This result indicates placement in *Target 360.*

1. can
2. pen
3. rack
4. hill
5. pond
6. nest
7. silk
~~8.~~ miten (mitten)
9. are
10. have
11. hurt
12. what
~~13.~~ blok (block)
~~14.~~ thinck (think)
~~15.~~ truck (trunk)

STOP TEST

This result indicates placement in *Target 540.*

1. can
2. pen
3. rack
4. hill
5. pond
6. nest
7. silk
8. mitten
9. are
10. have
11. hurt
12. what
13. block
14. think
15. trunk
~~16.~~ brantch (branch)
17. crash
18. shift
19. spend
20. strung
21. location
~~22.~~ stat (state)
~~23.~~ chare (chair)
24. judge
25. spoil
~~26.~~ brihgt (bright)

STOP TEST

Dictation Sentences

Lesson 1

1. She was **unaware** of my illness.
2. Smoking is **unhealthy**.
3. The two baseballs are **unequal** in size.
4. It is **unlikely** that the rain will stop.
5. The pond is **unsafe** for skating.
6. She was **unhappy** when it rained.
7. He believed the law to be **unjust**.
8. I am **uncertain** about my plans.

Lesson 2

1. The plane flew **nonstop** to Denver.
2. The idea seemed like **nonsense** to me.
3. I sat in the **nonsmoking** section.
4. She cooks with a **nonstick** pan.
5. Do you drink **nonfat** milk?
6. The store sold **nonliving** plants.
7. He enjoys reading **nonfiction** books.
8. The plastic jar is **nonbreakable**.

Lesson 3

1. Did you see the **preview** for that movie?
2. I will **precook** the ham.
3. The teacher gave us a **pretest**.
4. Do you know how to **prepare** shrimp?
5. My cousin goes to **preschool**.
6. **Preheat** the oven for your cake.
7. The insurance is **prepaid**.
8. I tried to **prevent** him from going.

Lesson 4

1. I go to my room when I want **peace**.
2. Please pass me a **piece** of cake.
3. **Some** of the boys like to camp.
4. What is the **sum** of those numbers?
5. She took a **bow** at the end of the show.
6. The **bough** of the tree broke in the wind.
7. Bend at the **waist** to do a dive.
8. Do not **waste** the food.

Lesson 5

1. I **dislike** eating beans.
2. I watched the balloon **disappear**.
3. He seems to always **disagree** with me.
4. Was that **dishonest**?
5. We got a great **discount** at the shop.
6. **Disconnect** the cord to the broken lamp.
7. We'll have to **disinfect** the wound.
8. Don't **disorganize** my thoughts.

Lesson 6

1. I like riding the **subway**.
2. The plant grew in **subzero** weather.
3. The temperature is **subfreezing**.
4. We live in a **suburban** area.
5. Have you ever seen a **submarine**?
6. The book had no **subtitle**.
7. The **subsoil** was filled with rocks.
8. **Submerge** a burn in cold water.

Lesson 7

1. I need to **refill** the tank.
2. We **recycle** newspaper and glass.
3. Please **review** the book.
4. She gave me a **refund**.
5. Do you know how to **repair** a watch?
6. It's time to **recharge** the battery.
7. They will **reclaim** land from the sea.
8. I will **rewind** the old clock.

Lesson 8

1. The **rain** poured down for days.
2. Hold the **rein** when you trot.
3. **Their** cat is nine years old.
4. We went **there** for a party.
5. My dad will **haul** hay today.
6. I walked down a long **hall**.
7. She has a **pair** of red socks.
8. He likes to eat a ripe **pear**.

Lesson 9

1. I will try not to **misplace** my gloves.
2. Did you see the **misprint** in the paper?
3. He tried to **mislead** us with a bad clue.
4. My dogs sometimes **misbehave**.
5. The queen didn't **mistreat** her people.
6. Do not **misuse** the tool.
7. It was my **misfortune** to insult the king.
8. Did you **misunderstand** me?

Lesson 10

1. We will sign the **contract** today.
2. Did you go to the **concert**?
3. Let's **congregate** at the park.
4. I have some **concern** for those animals.
5. He tried to **conform** to the rules.
6. You may **confide** in me.
7. Her parents gave their **consent**.
8. She will **conduct** the band.

Lesson 11

1. We will **descend** into the cave.
2. My grandmother can **dehydrate** apples.
3. They will pay the **deposit**.
4. It is time to **decide** where to go.
5. The size of the group will **decrease**.
6. The tire began to slowly **deflate**.
7. We will **depart** in the morning.
8. Can you **deliver** the paper for me?

Lesson 12

1. The queen sat on her **throne**.
2. The ball was **thrown** hard.
3. The sun **shone** brightly.
4. We were **shown** the way to the zoo.
5. The weather is **fair** today.
6. How much is the **fare** to town?
7. **It's** time to go skating.
8. The cat licked **its** fur.

Lesson 13

1. The snake is **harmless**.
2. The shot was **painless**.
3. Don't be **careless** with matches.
4. Finding a cure seemed **hopeless**.
5. That broken tool is **useless**.
6. The **helpless** kitten cried.
7. Her job is a **thankless** one.
8. His action was **thoughtless**.

Lesson 14

1. She was **thoughtful** toward her mother.
2. We live in a **peaceful** place.
3. Did you see the **beautiful** sunset?
4. That drug is **harmful**.
5. I am **careful** when I bike.
6. She is a **truthful** person.
7. We had some **hopeful** news.
8. I am **thankful** for your help.

Lesson 15

1. His **slowness** gave him time to think.
2. He had a terrible **sickness**.
3. I like the **coldness** of the cave.
4. The dusk left us in **darkness**.
5. He's known for his **fairness**.
6. Her **kindness** was easy to see.
7. The sky's **blackness** was strange.
8. I don't like the music's **loudness**.

Lesson 16

1. She likes **plain** pizza.
2. The **plane** flew over New York.
3. The bike race went **past** my house.
4. I **passed** the swim test.
5. The truck went back and **forth**.
6. She is in the **fourth** grade.
7. Put a **stake** at the corner of the tent.
8. We don't eat **steak** very often.

Lesson 17

1. He is a **friendly** person.
2. She stated her opinion **honestly**.
3. I tied the boat lines **correctly**.
4. The sky is **partly** cloudy.
5. Run **quickly** to the store.
6. We talked **quietly** while the baby slept.
7. They got out of the storm **safely**.
8. He **bravely** steered the bus to safety.

Lesson 18

1. I got a banking **statement** in the mail.
2. My brother and I had an **argument**.
3. We borrowed camping **equipment**.
4. That **payment** is due today.
5. The park is here for our **enjoyment**.
6. My parents are in a **retirement** home.
7. With your **encouragement** I'll do well.
8. I saw an **advertisement** for the movie.

Lesson 19

1. The **doe** came into the clearing.
2. We use **dough** to make bread.
3. I like to **peer** through store windows.
4. We fished off the **pier** at the beach.
5. The **air** from the north is cool.
6. I'm the **heir** to my grandmother's house.
7. He plays **bass** in the band.
8. She slid into first **base**.

Lesson 20

1. It's **possible** we'll go tonight.
2. Did you see that **horrible** film?
3. Those berries aren't **edible**.
4. The waterfall is **audible** a mile away.
5. We had a **terrible** fire last summer.
6. She had **incredible** energy.
7. The mountain is **visible** from here.
8. He was on a **sensible** diet.

Lesson 21

1. That cat is quite **likable**.
2. Do you think that story is **believable**?
3. The hammer is no longer **usable**.
4. I'm glad the chair is **returnable**.
5. Is that table **movable**?
6. My watch is not **valuable**.
7. Her dog is **lovable**.
8. The plate is **breakable**.

Lesson 22

1. My mother has so much **patience**.
2. The doctor saw twenty **patients** today.
3. She **threw** the ball to second base.
4. We went **through** the door.
5. **Who's** going to the game?
6. I don't know **whose** car that is.
7. **Your** hair is so long.
8. **You're** going to the beach today.

Lesson 23

1. Use **caution** when you cross the street.
2. Our **direction** now is south.
3. He had a broad **education**.
4. Laws are for everyone's **protection**.
5. She treated her nephew with **affection**.
6. The **operation** was a success.
7. His **transportation** was a train.
8. The house is under **construction**.

Lesson 24

1. The country suffered an **invasion**.
2. There was **confusion** after the storm.
3. I made a **decision** to stay home.
4. What's your favorite **television** show?
5. Her **vision** is perfect.
6. Did you hear the **explosion**?
7. The land has suffered **erosion**.
8. We were involved in a **collision**.

Lesson 25

1. The store underwent an **expansion**.
2. We had **permission** to hike there.
3. Our **mission** was to clear the trail.
4. **Tension** arose between the countries.
5. I'll need an **extension** cord.
6. The cost of **admission** was low.
7. It's not in my **possession**.
8. That story is beyond **comprehension**.

Lesson 26

1. The salt is very **coarse**.
2. My **course** of action is set.
3. Her **idol** was Abe Lincoln.
4. The dog was **idle** on the porch.
5. She tried in **vain** to reach her brother.
6. A **vein** on his forehead stood out.
7. He planned to **flee** by tunnel.
8. Did you see a **flea** jump?

Lesson 27

1. He had **confidence** in himself.
2. My surfing **experience** was fun.
3. I don't like **violence** on TV.
4. The **difference** between them is great.
5. The **conference** lasted three days.
6. We met on the plane by **coincidence**.
7. Her parents taught her **independence**.
8. No one questioned her **competence**.

Lesson 28

1. The **attendance** at school was high.
2. There was no **admittance** to the lake.
3. She was in charge of **finance**.
4. The **entrance** was between two trees.
5. The **endurance** contest lasted weeks.
6. Traffic stopped for the **ambulance**.
7. His face had a ghostly **appearance**.
8. The car's **performance** was flawless.

Lesson 29

1. I like your **company**.
2. Which **factory** makes the tables?
3. The story is a complex **mystery**.
4. Please accept my **apology**.
5. The book fair was held at the **library**.
6. The owl is the mouse's **enemy**.
7. Which **country** would you like to visit?
8. We're studying cell **biology** this week.

Lesson 30

1. The **principal** visits our classroom often.
2. He is a man of **principle**.
3. Would you be my **guest** this weekend?
4. I **guessed** the trees would sprout early.
5. Please say that **aloud** so I can hear it.
6. We're not **allowed** to go there.
7. I like the **presence** of the deer here.
8. She received many birthday **presents**.

Master Word List

The following spelling words presented in *Target Spelling* are listed in alphabetical order by book. The number after each word identifies the lesson in which the word is taught. See pages 135–140 in each student book for a lesson-by-lesson word list.

Target 180

a–1	brim–29	fast–17	lamp–12	new–24	rust–19	tent–16
all–17	bring–28	felt–21	land–14	no–26	sack–6	test–18
am–17	bump–13	fill–9	last–17	not–9	sad–2	that–28
an–1	but–20	find–3	lend–15	now–26	said–11	they–29
any–30	butter–20	fist–19	less–11	on–21	sand–14	this–29
are–18	came–11	flick–27	like–23	one–9	see–11	three–13
as–1	camp–12	fling–28	list–19	our–24	sell–8	tick–7
ask–23	can–1	fond–25	little–6	out–24	send–15	to–16
at–1	cast–17	for–14	lock–10	pack–6	sent–16	trap–26
ate–20	clap–26	funny–3	look–7	pen–4	she–27	trim–29
away–1	click–27	get–22	lump–13	pet–5	sick–7	two–13
bad–2	cling–28	go–14	mad–2	pick–7	silk–22	up–16
bag–3	come–2	good–22	make–7	pill–9	skim–29	wag–3
band–14	crop–30	hand–14	mask–23	play–10	slap–26	was–30
batter–20	dad–2	have–21	mast–17	please–25	slick–27	we–12
be–18	damp–12	he–4	me–8	pond–25	slim–29	well–8
bell–8	dent–16	help–5	melt–21	prop–30	so–27	went–16
belt–21	did–23	hen–4	mend–15	pump–13	sock–10	west–18
bend–15	do–23	here–5	mess–11	rack–6	soon–28	wet–5
best–18	dock–10	hill–9	milk–22	rag–3	sting–28	where–15
better–20	down–2	ill–9	mist–19	ramp–12	stop–30	wrap–26
big–4	drop–30	into–22	mitten–24	ran–25	tack–6	written–24
bitter–20	dump–13	jet–5	must–19	red–10	tag–3	yellow–15
blue–4	dust–19	jump–6	my–8	ride–25	task–23	you–12
bond–25	eat–21	kick–7	nest–18	rock–10	tell–8	
brick–27	elk–22	kitten–24	net–5	run–11	ten–4	

Target 360

about–16	cash–28	flash–28	lunch–28	scalp–4	spill–6	trust–11
after–11	champ–26	flesh–29	many–2	scan–4	stamp–6	try–3
again–11	chat–26	flip–2	melon–20	scrap–4	strap–10	twenty–27
always–29	check–26	flute–5	mind–20	scrub–4	string–10	twin–27
arm–7	chest–26	four–7	much–8	seldom–17	strung–13	under–22
bank–12	class–11	fresh–29	myself–8	seven–22	studied–21	use–17
basket–16	club–11	frog–9	never–6	shack–23	studies–21	visit–16
because–29	collar–14	full–14	off–21	shall–23	study–6	visitor–17
been–19	crack–8	glad–2	petal–19	shelf–23	swim–7	want–23
before–19	crash–8	glass–2	picnic–18	shell–23	swimming–7	warm–6
black–1	crush–30	goes–5	pinch–12	shift–24	swing–7	wash–2
blanket–16	crust–8	grab–9	plant–3	ship–24	swung–13	were–30
bled–1	cupful–22	grass–9	plenty–4	shock–24	table–30	what–25
blend–1	dish–29	group–10	plus–3	shop–24	thank–15	when–25
blink–14	doctor–17	handful–22	press–10	shut–25	their–18	which–25
block–1	does–24	hang–28	pretty–15	signal–19	there–20	white–25
book–7	dollar–14	happily–20	prompt–10	skate–21	these–15	who–27
both–24	done–9	helpful–22	quick–27	skill–5	think–15	will–27
bottle–19	drank–12	hive–16	quit–27	skin–21	those–15	wink–14
bottom–17	drink–9	hurt–14	rabbit–16	skunk–5	thunder–25	wish–29
branch–13	drum–9	hush–30	ranch–13	slept–3	today–13	with–26
brown–4	eight–15	inch–12	rush–30	slid–3	together–13	woman–1
brush–30	empty–18	junk–12	sadly–20	small–3	too–22	wonder–1
bunch–28	fifty–18	kind–8	sang–28	snack–5	traffic–18	yes–26
candle–19	first–23	laugh–10	saw–17	snap–5	trip–11	
carry–21	flag–2	lemon–20	say–18	spend–6	trunk–12	

Target 540

age–27	base–11	beard–30	bite–15	boat–9	brain–7	bright–27
arrow–21	beak–6	bee–1	blade–10	bore–22	brave–12	broke–16
art–20	beans–2	bike–13	board–30	born–22	bread–24	broom–8

(continued on next page)

Target 540 continued

brought–28
cage–27
cane–11
care–19
case–11
caught–28
chair–19
chance–26
chew–24
clean–2
clear–21
cloud–5
clown–3
coast–9
code–16
coin–4
cold–18
cool–8
could–30
dance–26
dark–20
deal–6
deer–21

dime–14
dirt–30
don't–18
draw–3
dream–6
drew–24
drive–15
drove–17
due–24
edge–26
every–30
face–25
fair–19
far–20
foot–1
flake–10
flame–12
floss–23
free–1
frown–3
fudge–26
give–2
glide–13

grape–11
grime–14
groom–8
ground–5
head–24
hear–21
heat–2
hedge–26
high–27
hold–18
home–16
how–3
ice–25
join–4
joke–16
joy–4
judge–26
knee–29
know–16
known–29
law–3
leap–6
life–13

light–27
live–23
load–9
location–25
long–23
mail–7
meet–1
mile–14
moon–8
narrow–21
note–17
oil–4
once–1
only–23
own–18
paid–7
pane–11
pave–12
peach–2
plain–7
plate–12
plow–3
pole–17

pound–5
price–25
pride–13
proud–5
read–2
real–6
ripe–15
road–9
rode–16
rose–17
scale–10
scar–20
scene–29
science–29
scout–5
scrape–11
shade–10
share–19
shark–20
sigh–27
skirt–30
slope–17
snake–10

snore–22
snow–18
space–25
spare–19
speak–6
spine–14
spoil–4
spoon–8
stare–19
start–20
state–12
station–25
steer–21
stone–17
strike–13
stripe–15
strong–23
tame–12
taught–28
though–28
thought–28
throat–9
through–28

throw–18
toast–9
tool–8
toss–23
toy–4
trail–7
trout–5
value–24
vine–14
wait–7
whale–10
while–14
why–15
wife–13
wise–15
world–22
worn–22
worth–22
wrinkle–29
write–29
your–1

Target 780

anybody–29
anyhow–29
anyone–29
anyplace–29
anything–29
anytime–29
anyway–29
anywhere–29
aren't–17
ate–9
August–3
axes–21
babies–23
bare–13
be–4
bear–13
bee–4
berries–23
blew–18
bloom–7
blue–18
booth–7
bosses–26
boxes–21
branches–22
breath–10
brief–8
brook–6
brushes–20
burn–2
burst–2
bushes–20
calves–25
catches–22
cause–3

cherries–23
chief–8
children–27
church–2
churches–22
cities–23
classes–26
claw–5
cook–6
crawl–5
crook–6
crushes–20
crutches–22
cry–12
curb–2
curve–2
dawn–5
didn't–17
dishes–20
doesn't–17
dresses–26
dry–12
early–11
earn–11
earth–11
eight–9
eighty–14
fault–3
fawn–5
feather–10
fern–1
field–8
fishes–20
fixes–21
flashes–20

flaw–5
flour–13
flower–13
fly–12
food–7
foot–6
for–13
four–13
foxes–21
freight–14
freighter–14
fry–12
gauze–3
geese–27
glasses–26
goose–7
guesses–26
guppies–23
hair–24
hare–24
hasn't–17
haul–3
haunt–3
heal–24
hear–18
heard–11
heavy–10
heel–24
he'll–19
her–1
herd–1
here–18
hood–6
hook–6
hour–28

I'll–19
illnesses–26
isn't–17
I've–19
jerk–1
kisses–26
knack–15
kneel–15
knew–18
knife–15
knight–15
knit–15
knives–25
knob–15
knock–15
knot–4
knot–15
know–28
launch–3
lawn–5
learn–11
leather–10
leaves–25
lives–25
loaves–25
loose–7
losses–26
made–4
maid–4
matches–22
men–27
mice–27
mixes–21
neigh–14
neighbor–14

nerve–1
new–18
niece–8
no–28
noon–7
not–4
nurse–2
our–28
oxen–27
pail–9
pale–9
pearl–11
pennies–23
perch–1
perk–1
piece–8
ponies–23
proof–7
pry–12
puppies–23
purse–2
read–4
ready–10
red–4
right–28
road–9
rode–9
sail–18
sale–18
scratches–22
sea–9
search–11
see–9
sew–24
sheep–27

she'll–19
shelves–25
shield–8
shy–12
sixes–21
sky–12
sleigh–14
somebody–30
someday–30
somehow–30
someone–30
someplace–30
something–30
sometime–30
somewhere–30
son–28
sow–24
speeches–22
spread–10
spy–12
stitches–22
stood–6
straw–5
sun–28
tail–24
tale–24
taxes–21
teeth–27
they've–19
thief–8
thieves–25
thread–10
to–13

tooth–7
turn–2
two–13
vault–3
verb–1
washes–20
wasn't–17
waxes–21
weather–10
weigh–14
weight–14
weren't–17
we've–19
wishes–20
wolves–25
women–27
won't–17
wood–6
wreath–16
wreck–16
wren–16
wrench–16
wrestle–16
wring–16
wrist–16
write–28
wrong–16
yawn–5
yearn–11
yield–8
you'll–19
you've–19

Target 1020

able–26
above–1
afraid–1
agree–1
alone–1

alphabet–13
amaze–1
ankle–25
another–3
apple–21

argue–18
around–1
avenue–18
avoid–1
awake–1

barrel–20
battle–24
beat–29
beet–29
beetle–24

bicycle–28
biting–5
bother–3
brake–23
break–23

brightest–15
brother–3
buckle–25
bugle–27
bushel–20

buy–8
by–8
cable–21
canned–11
canning–6

(continued on next page)

chapter–16
chased–10
cheaper–14
chimney–30
chopper–9
chuckle–25
cleanest–15
clever–16
clipper–9
closed–10
closet–2
clue–18
coming–5
continue–18
corner–16
cover–16
cradle–22
crinkle–25
cruel–20
dear–17
deer–17
dew–4
dial–19
diner–7
do–4
drizzle–28
dropped–11
dropper–9
dropping–6
duel–20

editorial–19
either–3
elephant–13
enter–16
example–28
fable–26
farther–3
father–3
fickle–25
filed–10
formal–19
fresher–14
fuel–20
fumble–26
gargle–27
gentle–24
geography–13
giggle–27
giver–7
glider–7
glue–18
gripping–6
handle–22
having–5
heard–12
herd–12
hiked–10
hockey–30
hole–8

hoping–5
hopped–11
hopping–6
humble–26
humming–6
jacket–2
jersey–30
jewel–20
jingle–27
jogger–9
journey–30
juggle–27
jungle–27
kettle–24
knight–4
knows–12
lead–23
led–23
living–5
loving–5
mail–8
making–5
male–8
maple–21
marble–26
market–2
meat–17
meet–17
metal–19
middle–22

monkey–30
mother–3
moved–10
mumble–26
neatest–15
needle–22
nephew–13
night–4
normal–19
nose–12
nozzle–28
older–14
one–17
other–3
pain–23
pane–23
pedal–19
peddle–22
people–21
personal–19
photo–13
phrase–13
pickle–25
pinning–6
pocket–2
poodle–22
pore–17
pour–17
pulley–30

purple–21
quicker–14
quickest–15
racket–2
rap–8
rattle–24
rescue–18
riddle–22
rifle–28
ripped–11
rocket–2
ruler–7
saddle–22
sample–28
scene–29
scraped–10
scrubbed–11
seen–29
settle–24
sharpest–15
shaver–7
shipped–11
shipping–6
shopper–9
sight–4
silver–16
simple–21
single–27
site–4
skater–7

slammed–11
slipper–9
smaller–14
smarter–14
socket–2
softest–15
sphere–13
stable–26
staple–21
statue–18
steal–29
steel–29
steeple–21
stepped–11
stopping–6
stronger–14
struggle–27
tackle–25
tattle–24
telephone–13
thicker–14
thimble–26
ticket–2
tickle–25
timed–10
title–24
towel–20
trial–19
true–18
turkey–30

used–10
using–5
valley–30
vehicle–28
voter–7
vowel–20
wade–4
waffle–28
wander–16
warmest–15
weak–29
wear–12
weather–12
week–29
weighed–4
where–12
whether–12
whisper–16
whole–8
winner–9
wiper–7
won–17
wood–23
would–23
wrap–8
zipper–9

admission–25
admittance–28
advertisement–18
affection–23
air–19
allowed–30
aloud–30
ambulance–28
apology–29
appearance–28
argument–18
attendance–28
audible–20
base–19
bass–19
beautiful–14
believable–21
biology–29
blackness–15
bough–4
bow–4
bravely–17
breakable–21
careful–14
careless–13
caution–23
coarse–26
coincidence–27
coldness–15
collision–24
company–29
competence–27

comprehension–25
concern–10
concert–10
conduct–10
conference–27
confide–10
confidence–27
conform–10
confusion–24
congregate–10
consent–10
construction–23
contract–10
correctly–17
country–29
course–26
darkness–15
decide–11
decision–24
decrease–11
deflate–11
dehydrate–11
deliver–11
depart–11
deposit–11
descend–11
difference–27
direction–23
disagree–5
disappear–5
disconnect–5
discount–5
dishonest–5
disinfect–5

dislike–5
disorganize–5
doe–19
dough–19
edible–20
education–23
encouragement–18
endurance–28
enemy–29
enjoyment–18
entrance–28
equipment–18
erosion–24
expansion–25
experience–27
explosion–24
extension–25
factory–29
fair–12
fairness–15
fare–12
finance–28
flea–26
flee–26
forth–16
fourth–16
friendly–17
guessed–30
guest–30
hall–8
harmful–14
harmless–13
haul–8
heir–19
helpless–13

honestly–17
hopeful–14
hopeless–13
horrible–20
idle–26
idol–26
incredible–20
independence–27
invasion–24
it's–12
its–12
kindness–15
library–29
likable–21
loudness–15
lovable–21
misbehave–9
misfortune–9
mislead–9
misplace–9
misprint–9
mission–25
mistreat–9
misunderstand–9
misuse–9
movable–21
mystery–29
nonbreakable–2
nonfat–2
nonfiction–2
nonliving–2
nonsense–2
nonsmoking–2

nonstick–2
nonstop–2
operation–23
painless–13
pair–8
partly–17
passed–16
past–16
patience–22
patients–22
payment–18
peace–4
peaceful–14
pear–8
peer–19
performance–28
permission–25
piece–4
pier–19
plain–16
plane–16
possession–25
possible–20
precook–3
preheat–3
prepaid–3
prepare–3
preschool–3
presence–30
presents–30
pretest–3
prevent–3
preview–3
principal–30
principle–30

protection–23
quickly–17
quietly–17
rain–8
recharge–7
reclaim–7
recycle–7
refill–7
refund–7
rein–8
repair–7
retirement–18
returnable–21
review–7
rewind–7
safely–17
sensible–20
shone–12
shown–12
sickness–15
slowness–15
some–4
stake–16
statement–18
steak–16
subfreezing–6
submarine–6
submerge–6
subsoil–6
subtitle–6
suburban–6
subway–6
subzero–6
sum–4
television–24
tension––25

terrible–20
thankful–14
thankless–13
their–8
there–8
thoughtful–14
thoughtless–13
threw–22
throne–12
through–22
thrown–12
transportation–23
truthful–14
unaware–1
uncertain–1
unequal–1
unhappy–1
unhealthy–1
unjust–1
unlikely–1
unsafe–1
usable–21
useless–13
vain–26
valuable–21
vein–26
violence–27
visible–20
vision–24
waist–4
waste–4
who's–22
whose–22
your–22
you're–22

Program Scope and Sequence

	Syllables/ Sight Words	Consonants/ Vowels	Word Meaning/ Usage	Word Analysis
TARGET 180 Reading Level: 1–2	• one-syllable words • sight words	• consonants and short vowels • consonant blends with short vowels • consonant digraphs • silent-letter combinations	• context clues	
TARGET 360 Reading Level: 2–3	• one-syllable words • two-syllable words • sight words	• consonants and short vowels • consonant blends with short vowels • consonant digraphs • silent-letter combinations	• context clues	
TARGET 540 Reading Level: 3	• one- and two-syllable words • three-syllable words • sight words	• consonants and long vowels • consonant blends with long vowels • consonant and vowel digraphs • diphthongs • silent-letter combinations	• context clues	
TARGET 780 Reading Level: 4	• one- and two-syllable words • three-syllable words	• consonant blends • consonant and vowel digraphs • diphthongs • silent-letter combinations • words with r-controlled vowels	• homonyms • context clues	• compound words • contractions • plurals
TARGET 1020 Reading Level: 5	• one- and two-syllable words • three-syllable words • four-syllable words	• consonant blends • consonant and vowel digraphs • diphthongs • silent-letter combinations	• homonyms • comparative/ superlative adjectives • context clues	• words with inflectional endings • words with -er as action agent
TARGET 1260 Reading Level: 6	• one- and two-syllable words • three-syllable words • four-syllable words	• consonant blends • consonant and vowel digraphs • diphthongs • silent-letter combinations	• homonyms • context clues	• compound words • words with inflectional endings • prefixes • suffixes

Word Study Sheet

(Make a check mark after each step.)

Words	1 Look at the Word	2 Say the Word	3 Think About Each Letter	4 Spell the Word Aloud	5 Write the Word	6 Check the Spelling	7 Repeat Steps (if needed)

Name _____

Checklist for Informal Assessment

Student's Name _____

Spelling Behaviors	Comments	Date
Readily attempts to spell new words		
Relies on a variety of strategies to spell new words		
Explains use of spelling strategies		
Recognizes and applies spelling patterns and word families		
Recognizes rhyming words		
Uses sound-symbol relationships to spell words		
Demonstrates understanding of segmenting words		
Uses inflectional endings		
Understands contractions		
Forms plurals		
Understands compound words		
Identifies homonyms		
Recognizes comparatives and superlatives		
Uses prefixes and suffixes		
Spells previously introduced high-frequency words correctly		
Understands meanings of spelling words		
Uses spelling words correctly in context		
Uses the dictionary		
Locates spelling errors in writing		
Corrects spelling errors in writing		
Maintains and refers to *My Word List*		
Consistently completes assigned spelling exercises		
Shows positive attitude toward spelling		
Explains why spelling is important		

T21

Student Progress Graph

(After each weekly test, you may wish to graph the number of words a student spells correctly.)

Number of words spelled correctly:

	Lesson 1	Lesson 2	Lesson 3	Lesson 4	Lesson 5	Lesson 6	Lesson 7	Lesson 8	Lesson 9	Lesson 10	Lesson 11	Lesson 12	Lesson 13	Lesson 14	Lesson 15	Lesson 16	Lesson 17	Lesson 18	Lesson 19	Lesson 20	Lesson 21	Lesson 22	Lesson 23	Lesson 24	Lesson 25	Lesson 26	Lesson 27	Lesson 28	Lesson 29	Lesson 30
8																														
7																														
6																														
5																														
4																														
3																														
2																														
1																														

Name _____

T22

Answer Key for Review and Test Practice Masters

Review for Lessons 1–5

T25
A.
1. un, non
2. nonbreakable
   disorganized
3. peace/piece
   bough/bow
   some/sum
   waist/waste

B. uncertain, prevent

4. unequal
   preview
   nonstick
   unhealthy
   disconnect
   nonliving

T26

C. Across	Down
1. nonstop	2. nonsense
4. disinfect	3. unjust
7. dishonest	5. unsafe
8. disagree	6. prepaid

Test Practice for Lessons 1–5

T27	**T28**
A.	**B.**
Example: B) unlikely	Example: D) prepare
1. C) nonstick	1. B) disinfect
2. B) unaware	2. C) bough
3. D) peace	3. A) preschool
4. A) nonfiction	4. C) dislike
5. C) nonstop	5. D) disconnect
6. B) unjust	6. B) waste
7. D) nonliving	7. C) prevent
8. C) unhealthy	8. D) discount
9. D) uncertain	9. B) preheat

Review for Lessons 6–10

T29
A.

reclaim	misplace	review
misfortune	recycle	misuse
subfreezing	submerge	

B. rain, haul, pair, their
C. suburban, subway, contract

T30

D. Across	Down
1. submarine	2. misunderstand
3. consent	4. mistreat
7. congregate	5. repair
8. concern	6. recharge

Test Practice for Lessons 6–10

T31	**T32**
A.	**B.**
Example: C) rewind	Example: C) misprint
1. B) repair	1. D) contract
2. A) submarine	2. B) mistreat
3. D) subway	3. D) pair
4. C) rain	4. D) mislead
5. D) subsoil	5. B) confide
6. B) recycle	6. C) consent
7. D) their	7. D) haul
8. C) submerge	8. C) misplace
9. D) review ɑʀ 🐝	9. D) concert

Review for Lessons 11–15

T33
A. painless, helpless, truthful, fairness, loudness, coldness
B. deliver, deposit, dehydrate, beautiful
C. thrown, it's, shone, fare
D. decide, deliver

T34

E. Across	Down
3. sickness	1. peaceful
5. thoughtful	2. blackness
7. slowness	4. thankful
8. descend	6. throne

F. Sentences may vary.

Test Practice for Lessons 11–15

T35	**T36**
A.	**B.**
Example: A) careless	Example: B) fair
1. B) descend	1. A) peaceful
2. C) deposit	2. C) darkness
3. C) shown	3. D) kindness
4. C) helpless	4. B) harmful
5. B) deliver	5. D) loudness
6. D) harmless	6. B) blackness
7. C) decide	7. C) beautiful
8. D) thrown	8. A) hopeful
9. C) decrease	9. C) it's

Review for Lessons 16–20

T37

A. 1. passed, possible, correctly, terrible, bass horrible
2. friendly, argument, sensible, fourth
3. plain, heir, steak, pier

B. past, quickly, enjoyment

T38

C.

Across	Down
1. audible	1. advertisement
3. doe	2. edible
6. quietly	4. equipment
7. visible	5. plane
9. heir	8. base
10. stake	
11. honestly	

Test Practice for Lessons 16–20

T39

A.

Example: C) bravely
1. D) quickly
2. B) steak
3. D) friendly
4. B) forth
5. A) partly
6. C) past
7. B) dough
8. C) pier
9. B) plain

T40

B.

Example: C) equipment
1. D) edible
2. C) heir
3. D) bass
4. C) horrible
5. B) sensible
6. D) argument
7. A) enjoyment
8. C) incredible
9. B) advertisement

Review for Lessons 21–25

T41

A. 1. who's, you're
2. whose, you're, threw
3. affection, expansion, confusion, lovable decision
4. construction, transportation, comprehension
5. returnable, breakable

B. through, collision, vision, protection

T42

C.

Across	Down
3. whose	1. usable
5. valuable	2. your
7. believable	4. collision
9. admission	6. extension
10. through	8. invasion
11. threw	

Test Practice for Lessons 21–25

T43

A.

Example: B) operation
1. C) usable
2. D) through
3. D) direction
4. A) affection
5. B) valuable
6. C) patients
7. C) caution
8. B) lovable
9. C) movable

T44

B.

Example: C) decision
1. D) admission
2. B) vision
3. D) erosion
4. D) who's
5. B) mission
6. C) invasion
7. C) you're
8. D) tension
9. A) collision

Review for Lessons 26–30

T45

A. 1. guessed, presents, course, vein, idol
2. confidence, admittance, endurance, performance, competence, independence
3. coincidence, biology, apology, experience, independence

B. attendance, biology, library

T46

C.

Across	Down
3. mystery	1. company
5. appearance	2. principal
7. coarse	4. vain
8. difference	6. ambulance

D. Sentences may vary.

Test Practice for Lessons 26–30

T47

A.

Example: C) entrance
1. C) violence
2. B) difference
3. A) finance
4. C) coarse
5. D) idle
6. D) confidence
7. C) ambulance
8. D) course
9. C) idol

T48

B.

Example: C) library
1. B) factory
2. C) vain
3. D) mystery
4. B) presence
5. D) country
6. D) allowed
7. C) principle
8. D) guest
9. A) apology

Review for Lessons 1–5

 A **Fill in each blank with a spelling word.**

1. Write the two prefixes that can mean "not."

   _____   _____

2. Write the spelling words that have four syllables.

   _____   _____

3. Write the four pairs of homonyms.

   _____   _____

   _____   _____

   _____   _____

   _____   _____

4. Write the spelling words that come from these root words.

   equal   _____

   view   _____

   stick   _____

   health   _____

   connect   _____

   live   _____

B **Use spelling words to complete the story.**

Our school had a picnic the first weekend in May. Spring

weather is always _____, so we put up a tent

to _____ us from getting wet if it rained. The

morning was cloudy. But by noon the sun had burned the

clouds from the sky. It turned out to be a great day for a

picnic.

Name _____

T25

unaware
unhealthy
unequal
unlikely
unsafe
unhappy
unjust
uncertain
nonstop
nonsense
nonsmoking
nonstick
nonfat
nonliving
nonfiction
nonbreakable
preview
precook
pretest
prepare
preschool
preheat
prepaid
prevent
peace
piece
some
sum
bow
bough
waist
waste
dislike
disappear
disagree
dishonest
discount
disconnect
disinfect
disorganize

Review for Lessons 1–5

C Use spelling words to complete the puzzle.

Across

1. without stopping

4. to get rid of germs

7. not honest

8. to hold a different opinion

Down

2. something that doesn't make sense

3. not fair

5. not safe

6. paid earlier

unaware
unhealthy
unequal
unlikely
unsafe
unhappy
unjust
uncertain
nonstop
nonsense
nonsmoking
nonstick
nonfat
nonliving
nonfiction
nonbreakable
preview
precook
pretest
prepare
preschool
preheat
prepaid
prevent
peace
piece
some
sum
bow
bough
waist
waste
dislike
disappear
disagree
dishonest
discount
disconnect
disinfect
disorganize

Name _____

Test Practice for Lessons 1–5

 A Read each sentence. Find the correctly spelled word to complete it. Shade the letter next to the word.

EXAMPLE

It seemed _____ that it would rain.

Ⓐ unlikly   ●Ⓑ unlikely   Ⓒ umlikely   Ⓓ unliekly

---

1. "Do you like using a _____ frying pan?" she asked.

Ⓐ nonstich   Ⓑ nonsitck   Ⓒ nonstick   Ⓓ nonsticke

2. He was _____ of the danger.

Ⓐ unawrae   Ⓑ unaware   Ⓒ unawaer   Ⓓ umawear

3. We like _____ instead of conflict.

Ⓐ pease   Ⓑ peaec   Ⓒ paece   Ⓓ peace

4. I like reading _____ books.

Ⓐ nonfiction   Ⓑ nonfictoin   Ⓒ nonfictione   Ⓓ nonefiction

5. Our plane made a _____ flight to Florida.

Ⓐ nonstoep   Ⓑ nonstope   Ⓒ nonstop   Ⓓ nonstap

6. The new rules are unnecessary and _____.

Ⓐ unjuts   Ⓑ unjust   Ⓒ unjuste   Ⓓ ungust

7. Though _____, fossils have much to teach us.

Ⓐ nonliwing   Ⓑ nonlivimg   Ⓒ nonliveing   Ⓓ nonliving

8. Studies show smoking is _____.

Ⓐ unhealhty   Ⓑ unhaelthy   Ⓒ unhealthy   Ⓓ unhelthy

9. His vacation plans were _____.

Ⓐ uncertian   Ⓑ uncerlain   Ⓒ uncretain   Ⓓ uncertain

Name _____

Test Practice for Lessons 1–5

B Find the correctly spelled word to complete each phrase. Shade the letter next to the correct word.

EXAMPLE

_____ for the test

Ⓐ perpare   Ⓑ prepaer   Ⓒ prepear   ⬤ prepare

---

1. _____ the bathroom

   Ⓐ disinfec   Ⓑ disinfect   Ⓒ disenfect   Ⓓ disnifect

2. _____ of the tree

   Ⓐ bouhg   Ⓑ bowgh   Ⓒ bough   Ⓓ boegh

3. attend the _____

   Ⓐ preschool   Ⓑ perschool   Ⓒ preshcool   Ⓓ preeschool

4. _____ that food

   Ⓐ dislick   Ⓑ disliek   Ⓒ dislike   Ⓓ dislicke

5. _____ the wire

   Ⓐ disconneck   Ⓑ disconncet   Ⓒ disconect   Ⓓ disconnect

6. _____ not; want not

   Ⓐ waest   Ⓑ waste   Ⓒ waset   Ⓓ vaste

7. _____ a forest fire

   Ⓐ prevint   Ⓑ preevent   Ⓒ prevent   Ⓓ pervent

8. bought at a _____

   Ⓐ disconut   Ⓑ discout   Ⓒ discouwnt   Ⓓ discount

9. _____ the oven

   Ⓐ perheat   Ⓑ preheat   Ⓒ prehaet   Ⓓ preheet

Name _____

Review for Lessons 6–10

A Write the spelling words that come from these root words.

claim   _____

fortune   _____

freeze   _____

place   _____

cycle   _____

merge   _____

view   _____

use   _____

B Write the spelling words that are homonyms for the words below.

rein   _____

hall   _____

pear   _____

there   _____

C Use spelling words to complete the story.

We used to live right in town, but we moved to a

_____ neighborhood. My parents wanted to be

closer to the lake.

When we lived in town, my dad always took the

_____ to work. Now he's in a carpool with four

other people. They signed a kind of _____.

Each person drives the carpool one day a week.

subway
subzero
subfreezing
suburban
submarine
subtitle
subsoil
submerge
refill
recycle
review
refund
repair
recharge
reclaim
rewind
rain
rein
their
there
haul
hall
pair
pear
misplace
misprint
mislead
misbehave
mistreat
misuse
misfortune
misunderstand
contract
concert
congregate
concern
conform
confide
consent
conduct

Name _____

Review for Lessons 6–10

 D Use spelling words to complete the puzzle.

Across	Down
1. a ship that can go under water	**2.** to not understand
3. to agree to something	**4.** to treat wrongly
7. to get together	**5.** fix
8. worry	**6.** to charge again

subway
subzero
subfreezing
suburban
submarine
subtitle
subsoil
submerge
refill
recycle
review
refund
repair
recharge
reclaim
rewind
rain
rein
their
there
haul
hall
pair
pear
misplace
misprint
mislead
misbehave
mistreat
misuse
misfortune
misunderstand
contract
concert
congregate
concern
conform
confide
consent
conduct

Name _____

Test Practice for Lessons 6–10

 A Read each sentence. Find the correctly spelled word to complete it. Shade the letter next to the word.

EXAMPLE

Please _____ the movie.

(A) rewinde   (B) rewine   (C) rewind   (D) rewiend

---

1. I need to _____ my bike.

   (A) repiar   (B) repair   (C) repare   (D) repaer

2. Have you ever been on a _____?

   (A) submarine   (B) subnamine   (C) submarien   (D) submareen

3. I rode the _____ in New York once.

   (A) subwaey   (B) subwaye   (C) subwayye   (D) subway

4. "The sky is turning dark, and it looks like it may _____," he said.

   (A) rein   (B) rian   (C) rain   (D) rane

5. The _____ here is clay.

   (A) subsole   (B) subsiol   (C) subsoyl   (D) subsoil

6. It's important to _____ as much as possible.

   (A) recycel   (B) recycle   (C) recylce   (D) recicle

7. I like _____ suburban home.

   (A) thier   (B) there   (C) they're   (D) their

8. To cook rice, you must _____ it in water.

   (A) submerje   (B) submrege   (C) submerge   (D) submerg

9. I need to _____ the facts before I decide.

   (A) reveue   (B) review   (C) revue   (D) review

Name _____

Test Practice for Lessons 6–10

 B **Find the correctly spelled word to complete each phrase. Shade the letter next to the correct word.**

> **EXAMPLE**
>
> _____ on the invitation
>
> Ⓐ mispirnt   Ⓑ misprient   ⬤Ⓒ misprint   Ⓓ misprin

1. _____ for work

Ⓐ contarct   Ⓑ contrac   Ⓒ contrakt   Ⓓ contract

2. did not _____ the animal

Ⓐ mistraet   Ⓑ mistreat   Ⓒ misterat   Ⓓ miztreat

3. _____ of socks

Ⓐ pear   Ⓑ pare   Ⓒ piar   Ⓓ pair

4. _____ the witness

Ⓐ mislaed   Ⓑ misleade   Ⓒ mislede   Ⓓ mislead

5. _____ in a friend

Ⓐ confied   Ⓑ confide   Ⓒ conefide   Ⓓ confiede

6. _____ to leave now

Ⓐ concent   Ⓑ consennt   Ⓒ consent   Ⓓ consint

7. _____ the trash outside

Ⓐ hall   Ⓑ holl   Ⓒ hale   Ⓓ haul

8. _____ the keys

Ⓐ mispalce   Ⓑ misplase   Ⓒ misplace   Ⓓ misplaec

9. meet at the _____

Ⓐ consert   Ⓑ conserte   Ⓒ consurt   Ⓓ concert

Name _____

Review for Lessons 11–15

A **Write the spelling words that come from these root words.**

pain _____

help _____

truth _____

fair _____

loud _____

cold _____

B **Write the spelling words that have three syllables.**

_____   _____

_____   _____

C **Write the spelling words that are homonyms for the words below.**

throne _____

its _____

shown _____

fair _____

D **Use spelling words to complete the story.**

I want to do something nice for my friend, but I can't

_____ what to do. Should I mail her a nice

card? Or should I _____ some flowers to her

house? I know that she will like either one.

descend
dehydrate
deposit
decide
decrease
deflate
depart
deliver
throne
thrown
shone
shown
fair
fare
it's
its
harmless
painless
careless
hopeless
useless
helpless
thankless
thoughtless
thoughtful
peaceful
beautiful
harmful
careful
truthful
hopeful
thankful
slowness
sickness
coldness
darkness
fairness
kindness
blackness
loudness

Name _____

T33

Review for Lessons 11–15

 E **Use spelling words to complete the puzzle.**

Across

3. illness

5. having thoughts

7. opposite of "fastness"

8. to go down

Down

1. filled with peace

2. darkness

4. grateful

6. a royal chair

| descend |
| dehydrate |
| deposit |
| decide |
| decrease |
| deflate |
| depart |
| deliver |
| throne |
| thrown |
| shone |
| shown |
| fair |
| fare |
| it's |
| its |
| harmless |
| painless |
| careless |
| hopeless |
| useless |
| helpless |
| thankless |
| thoughtless |
| thoughtful |
| peaceful |
| beautiful |
| harmful |
| careful |
| truthful |
| hopeful |
| thankful |
| slowness |
| sickness |
| coldness |
| darkness |
| fairness |
| kindness |
| blackness |
| loudness |

F **Use spelling words in two sentences.**

_____

_____

T34

Name _____

Test Practice for Lessons 11–15

 Read each sentence. Find the correctly spelled word to complete it. Shade the letter next to the word.

EXAMPLE

She acted in a _____ manner.

Ⓐ careless   Ⓑ caerless   Ⓒ kareless   Ⓓ cairless

---

1. "When will he _____ the staircase?" the woman asked.

Ⓐ desend   Ⓑ descend   Ⓒ descemd   Ⓓ descenb

2. I'm going to the bank to _____ the paycheck.

Ⓐ depawsit   Ⓑ depozit   Ⓒ deposit   Ⓓ deposet

3. He had _____ great kindness to the lost kitten.

Ⓐ showen   Ⓑ showne   Ⓒ shown   Ⓓ shone

4. It seemed thoughtless to ignore the _____ animal.

Ⓐ helples   Ⓑ hepless   Ⓒ helpless   Ⓓ helplass

5. My morning job is to _____ the newspaper.

Ⓐ delivir   Ⓑ deliver   Ⓒ delever   Ⓓ delivre

6. A bite by that _____ spider is painless.

Ⓐ harmles   Ⓑ harmlass   Ⓒ hermless   Ⓓ harmless

7. It's time to _____ whether to leave or stay.

Ⓐ deside   Ⓑ deciede   Ⓒ decide   Ⓓ diside

8. The ball was _____ a great distance.

Ⓐ throne   Ⓑ throene   Ⓒ throen   Ⓓ thrown

9. Let's _____ the amount of energy that we each use.

Ⓐ decrese   Ⓑ decreese   Ⓒ decrease   Ⓓ dekrese

Name _____

Test Practice for Lessons 11–15

B **Find the correctly spelled word to complete each phrase. Shade the letter next to the correct word.**

EXAMPLE

ride at the _____

Ⓐ fare   🅱 fair   Ⓒ faer   Ⓓ fayr

1. in the _____ countryside

Ⓐ peaceful   Ⓑ peaseful   Ⓒ peacefull   Ⓓ pieceful

2. _____ of the night

Ⓐ darknes   Ⓑ darcness   Ⓒ darkness   Ⓓ darkeness

3. a grandmother's _____

Ⓐ kindnezz   Ⓑ kindeness   Ⓒ kineness   Ⓓ kindness

4. _____ rays of the sun

Ⓐ harmfull   Ⓑ harmful   Ⓒ harmeful   Ⓓ hermful

5. _____ of the radio

Ⓐ lowdness   Ⓑ loudnes   Ⓒ loudnezz   Ⓓ loudness

6. _____ of the night

Ⓐ blachness   Ⓑ blackness   Ⓒ blakness   Ⓓ blacness

7. _____ smiles of children

Ⓐ beuatiful   Ⓑ beauteful   Ⓒ beautiful   Ⓓ beautifull

8. a future for _____ candidates

Ⓐ hopeful   Ⓑ hopefull   Ⓒ hoapful   Ⓓ hopefal

9. hope _____ raining

Ⓐ its'   Ⓑ i'ts   Ⓒ it's   Ⓓ itts

Name _____

Review for Lessons 16–20

 A **Fill in each blank with a spelling word.**

1. Write the words with double consonants.

_____   _____

_____   _____

_____   _____

2. Write the words that come from these root words.

friend   _____

argue   _____

sense   _____

four   _____

3. Write the words that are homonyms for the words below.

plane   _____

air   _____

stake   _____

peer   _____

B **Use spelling words to complete the story.**

My brother and I went skiiing for the first time. My brother

had a hard time learning at first. He practiced all day long. All

of a sudden, I saw someone ski _____ me. I

_____ turned my head to see who it was. It was

my brother! He was having fun. I could see the _____

on his face.

plain
plane
past
passed
forth
fourth
stake
steak
friendly
honestly
correctly
partly
quickly
quietly
safely
bravely
statement
argument
equipment
payment
enjoyment
retirement
encouragement
advertisement
doe
dough
peer
pier
air
heir
bass
base
possible
horrible
edible
audible
terrible
incredible
visible
sensible

Name _____

Review for Lessons 16–20

 C   **Use spelling words to complete the puzzle.**

Across

1. able to be heard
3. female deer
6. without loudness
7. something that can be seen
9. someone who inherits something
10. a pointed piece of wood
11. truthfully

Down

1. an ad
2. something that can be eaten
4. machines to help with work
5. a vehicle that travels through the air
8. the bottom of

plain
plane
past
passed
forth
fourth
stake
steak
friendly
honestly
correctly
partly
quickly
quietly
safely
bravely
statement
argument
equipment
payment
enjoyment
retirement
encouragement
advertisement
doe
dough
peer
pier
air
heir
bass
base
possible
horrible
edible
audible
terrible
incredible
visible
sensible

Name _____

Test Practice for Lessons 16–20

 A Read each sentence. Find the correctly spelled word to complete it. Shade the letter next to the word.

EXAMPLE

The dog ran _____ to the scared child.

Ⓐ bravly   Ⓑ bravley   ● bravely   Ⓓ braevly

---

1. She ran _____ to the swing.

Ⓐ quikly   Ⓑ quickley   Ⓒ quicly   Ⓓ quickly

2. How do you like your _____ to be cooked?

Ⓐ stake   Ⓑ steak   Ⓒ staek   Ⓓ stack

3. "The people in this town are very _____," I said.

Ⓐ freindly   Ⓑ friemdly   Ⓒ frindley   Ⓓ friendly

4. The dog paced back and _____.

Ⓐ forthe   Ⓑ forth   Ⓒ foreth   Ⓓ forht

5. That answer is _____ correct.

Ⓐ partly   Ⓑ paretly   Ⓒ partley   Ⓓ partlie

6. We drove _____ the store.

Ⓐ passt   Ⓑ pased   Ⓒ past   Ⓓ paste

7. Do you know how to make the cookie _____?

Ⓐ douhg   Ⓑ dough   Ⓒ doegh   Ⓓ dowgh

8. We sat on the _____ to watch the sailboats.

Ⓐ peer   Ⓑ pere   Ⓒ pier   Ⓓ peir

9. I prefer _____ cars to fancy ones.

Ⓐ plane   Ⓑ plain   Ⓒ plaen   Ⓓ plaine

Name _____

Test Practice for Lessons 16–20

B   **Find the correctly spelled word to complete each phrase. Shade the letter next to the correct word.**

EXAMPLE

_____ for the camping trip

Ⓐ eqipment   Ⓑ equipmint   Ⓒ equipment   Ⓓ ecuipment

---

1. an _____ mushroom

Ⓐ edibel   Ⓑ edeble   Ⓒ eadible   Ⓓ edible

2. _____ to a fortune

Ⓐ hier   Ⓑ air   Ⓒ heir   Ⓓ here

3. sing the _____ line

Ⓐ base   Ⓑ bace   Ⓒ bast   Ⓓ bass

4. scene of a _____ accident

Ⓐ horible   Ⓑ horribel   Ⓒ horrible   Ⓓ horrebil

5. a _____ way to live

Ⓐ senseble   Ⓑ sensible   Ⓒ sencible   Ⓓ sensebel

6. for the sake of _____

Ⓐ arqument   Ⓑ arguemen   Ⓒ argumnet   Ⓓ argument

7. hobbies for _____

Ⓐ enjoyment   Ⓑ enjoiment   Ⓒ enjoymen   Ⓓ injoyment

8. an _____ experience

Ⓐ incridible   Ⓑ encredible   Ⓒ incredible   Ⓓ incredibel

9. _____ in the paper

Ⓐ advertizement   Ⓑ advertisement   Ⓒ advirtisement   Ⓓ advertisemint

Name _____

Review for Lessons 21–25

A   **Fill in each blank with a spelling word.**

1. _____ and _____ are contractions.

2. _____, _____, and _____ are the
   only words with five letters.

3. Write the words that come from these root words.

   affect   _____

   expand   _____

   confuse   _____

   love   _____

   decide   _____

4. The three longest words are _____,

   _____, and _____.

5. Of the words ending in *able*, which two do <u>not</u> have a final
   e dropped?

   _____   _____

B   **Use spelling words to complete the story.**

Last week I was in a car accident. I was driving

_____ an intersection, when another car

ran a red light and hit the side of my car.

There was no way to avoid the _____.

I bumped my head on the rearview mirror. For a while, I felt

dizzy and had double _____. Then I felt all

right. I'm glad I had a seatbelt on for _____.

likable
believable
usable
returnable
movable
valuable
lovable
breakable
patience
patients
threw
through
who's
whose
your
you're
caution
direction
education
protection
affection
operation
transportation
construction
invasion
confusion
decision
television
vision
explosion
erosion
collision
expansion
permission
mission
tension
extension
admission
possession
comprehension

Name _____

Review for Lessons 21–25

C Use spelling words to complete the puzzle.

Across

3. ___ book is this?
5. worth a lot
7. capable of being believed
9. an entrance fee
10. in one side and out the other
11. He ___ the ball to first base.

Down

1. capable of being used
2. belonging to you
4. a crash
6. an increase in length
8. entrance by force

likable
believable
usable
returnable
movable
valuable
lovable
breakable
patience
patients
threw
through
who's
whose
your
you're
caution
direction
education
protection
affection
operation
transportation
construction
invasion
confusion
decision
television
vision
explosion
erosion
collision
expansion
permission
mission
tension
extension
admission
possession
comprehension

Name _____

Test Practice for Lessons 21–25

 A Read each sentence. Find the correctly spelled word to complete it. Shade the letter next to the word.

EXAMPLE

The _____ lasted for six hours.

Ⓐ operatoin   ● operation   Ⓒ opuration   Ⓓ opreation

---

1. Nearly everything is _____.

Ⓐ usabel   Ⓑ uzable   Ⓒ usable   Ⓓ useable

2. We hiked _____ the canyon.

Ⓐ thrue   Ⓑ threw   Ⓒ thruegh   Ⓓ through

3. Which _____ is the train station?

Ⓐ directoin   Ⓑ direktion   Ⓒ direcshun   Ⓓ direction

4. My cat always shows me a lot of _____.

Ⓐ affection   Ⓑ afection   Ⓒ affectoin   Ⓓ afectshun

5. I learned a _____ lesson.

Ⓐ valueable   Ⓑ valuable   Ⓒ valuabel   Ⓓ valuoble

6. The nurse cared for many _____.

Ⓐ patiens   Ⓑ pateints   Ⓒ patients   Ⓓ patientz

7. "We must exercise _____ in this situation," they told us.

Ⓐ cautoin   Ⓑ cawtion   Ⓒ caution   Ⓓ caushun

8. He is a _____ character.

Ⓐ loveable   Ⓑ lovable   Ⓒ loveble   Ⓓ lovabel

9. This table is not _____.

Ⓐ moveable   Ⓑ moovable   Ⓒ movable   Ⓓ moveble

Name _____

Test Practice for Lessons 21–25

B Find the correctly spelled word to complete each phrase. Shade the letter next to the correct word.

EXAMPLE

make a _____

(A) desision   (B) decisoin   ● (C) decision   (D) decishion

---

1. _____ to the concert

(A) admision   (B) admishion   (C) addmission   (D) admission

2. _____ of the future

(A) vizion   (B) vision   (C) viseion   (D) visoin

3. _____ of the river banks

(A) erozion   (B) erosun   (C) eroshion   (D) erosion

4. _____ there

(A) wh'os   (B) whos'   (C) who'se   (D) who's

5. outer space _____

(A) mision   (B) mission   (C) mishion   (D) missoin

6. _____ of privacy

(A) invaseion   (B) invasun   (C) invasion   (D) invasoin

7. _____ the one

(A) your'e   (B) youre'   (C) you're   (D) you'r

8. _____ at the event

(A) tinsion   (B) tenshun   (C) tensoin   (D) tension

9. _____ of the cars

(A) collision   (B) colision   (C) collsion   (D) collition

Name _____

Review for Lessons 26–30

 A **Fill in each blank with a spelling word.**

1. Write the words that are homonyms for the words below.

   guest   _____

   presence   _____

   coarse   _____

   vain   _____

   idle   _____

2. Write the words that come from these root words.

   confide   _____

   admit   _____

   endure   _____

   perform   _____

   compete   _____

   depend   _____

3. Write the words that have four syllables.

   _____   _____

   _____   _____

   _____

B **Use spelling words to complete the story.**

My sister is in high school. She has not missed any days of

school this year. She's hoping for a perfect _____

record. She studies English, math, and _____. She

also works in the _____ at her school.

| coarse |
| course |
| idol |
| idle |
| vain |
| vein |
| flee |
| flea |
| confidence |
| experience |
| violence |
| difference |
| conference |
| coincidence |
| independence |
| competence |
| attendance |
| admittance |
| finance |
| entrance |
| endurance |
| ambulance |
| appearance |
| performance |
| company |
| factory |
| mystery |
| apology |
| library |
| enemy |
| country |
| biology |
| principal |
| principle |
| guest |
| guessed |
| aloud |
| allowed |
| presence |
| presents |

Name _____

Review for Lessons 26–30

 C Use spelling words to complete the puzzle.

Across

3. a puzzling occurrence

5. the way something looks

7. rough

8. a change between two things

Down

1. a business or corporation

2. the leader of a school

4. proud to a fault

6. vehicle for medical emergencies

D Use spelling words in two sentences.

_____

_____

Name _____

coarse
course
idol
idle
vain
vein
flee
flea
confidence
experience
violence
difference
conference
coincidence
independence
competence
attendance
admittance
finance
entrance
endurance
ambulance
appearance
performance
company
factory
mystery
apology
library
enemy
country
biology
principal
principle
guest
guessed
aloud
allowed
presence
presents

Test Practice for Lessons 26–30

 A Read each sentence. Find the correctly spelled word to complete it. Shade the letter next to the word.

EXAMPLE

There is no admittance at the north _____.

(A) entrince   (B) entrence   (C) entrance   (D) entarnce

1. We heard about the _____ yesterday.

(A) violince   (B) vilance   (C) violence   (D) violense

2. "Can you hear the _____ in the bird calls?" my dad asked.

(A) diference   (B) difference   (C) diffrence   (D) differance

3. The _____ committee will meet today.

(A) finance   (B) finanse   (C) fineance   (D) finence

4. The _____ hair helps the animal to endure the cold weather.

(A) corese   (B) coaurse   (C) coarse   (D) coars

5. It can be relaxing to be _____ sometimes.

(A) idil   (B) idel   (C) idal   (D) idle

6. She showed great _____ in her performance.

(A) conefidence   (B) confedence   (C) confidense   (D) confidence

7. When did the _____ appear?

(A) anbulance   (B) ambulence   (C) ambulance   (D) ambuelance

8. Of _____, I will meet you at the movie tonight.

(A) coarse   (B) cores   (C) coures   (D) course

9. I went to the concert to see a music _____.

(A) idle   (B) idal   (C) idol   (D) idole

Name _____

Test Practice for Lessons 26–30

B **Find the correctly spelled word to complete each phrase. Shade the letter next to the correct word.**

EXAMPLE

research at the _____

Ⓐ liebrary   Ⓑ libary   Ⓒ library   Ⓓ librery

---

1. change jobs at the _____

Ⓐ factroy   Ⓑ factory   Ⓒ faktory   Ⓓ factery

2. try in _____

Ⓐ vaine   Ⓑ vane   Ⓒ vain   Ⓓ vaen

3. will always be a _____

Ⓐ mistery   Ⓑ mystary   Ⓒ mystrey   Ⓓ mystery

4. felt a great _____

Ⓐ presenze   Ⓑ presence   Ⓒ presense   Ⓓ presance

5. enemy of the _____

Ⓐ countrie   Ⓑ contry   Ⓒ countree   Ⓓ country

6. no pets _____

Ⓐ alloued   Ⓑ alowed   Ⓒ allouwed   Ⓓ allowed

7. _____ by which he lives

Ⓐ principel   Ⓑ princeple   Ⓒ principle   Ⓓ prinsiple

8. a _____ coming to dinner

Ⓐ guesst   Ⓑ gest   Ⓒ gueste   Ⓓ guest

9. offer an _____

Ⓐ apology   Ⓑ apolgy   Ⓒ apalogy   Ⓓ apolagy

Name _____

Steck Vaughn

Target Spelling 1260

Margaret Scarborough
Mary F. Brigham
Teresa A. Miller

Harcourt Achieve

Rigby • Steck-Vaughn

www.HarcourtAchieve.com
1.800.531.5015

Table of Contents

Acknowledgment
Cover Illustration by Dan Clayton

ISBN 0-7398-9193-6

1 2 3 4 5 6 7 8 059 11 10 09 08 07 06 05 04

Word Study Plan

1 **LOOK** at the word. _____

2 **SAY** the word. _____

3 **THINK** about each letter. _____

4 **SPELL** the word aloud. _____

5 **WRITE** the word. _____

6 **CHECK** the spelling. _____

7 **REPEAT** the steps
if you need more practice. _____

Name _____

1

Spelling Strategies

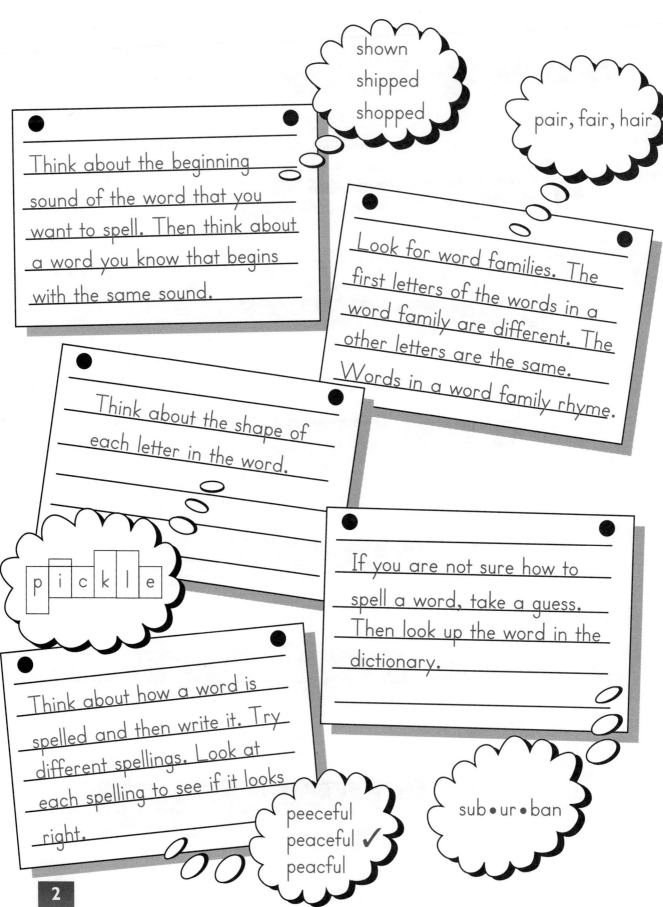

shown
shipped
shopped

pair, fair, hair

Think about the beginning sound of the word that you want to spell. Then think about a word you know that begins with the same sound.

Look for word families. The first letters of the words in a word family are different. The other letters are the same. Words in a word family rhyme.

Think about the shape of each letter in the word.

p i c k l e

If you are not sure how to spell a word, take a guess. Then look up the word in the dictionary.

Think about how a word is spelled and then write it. Try different spellings. Look at each spelling to see if it looks right.

peeceful
peaceful ✓
peacful

sub•ur•ban

Lesson 1

Words with *un-*

| unaware | unequal | unsafe | unjust |
| unhealthy | unlikely | unhappy | uncertain |

A Circle the spelling word. Then write it on the line.
(The prefix *un* means "not.")

1. He felt (unhappy) when his team lost the game. **unhappy**

2. The ice was (unsafe) for skating. _____unsafe_____

3. Today the weather is (uncertain.) _____uncertain_____

4. The pie was divided into (unequal) pieces. _____unequal_____

5. The person's remarks seemed (unjust.) _____unjust_____

6. (Unaware) of the storm, she began hiking up the trail. _____unaware_____

7. Doctors have said that smoking is (unhealthy) for people. _____unhealthy_____

8. It seems (unlikely) that it will rain today. _____unlikely_____

B Circle the word that is the same as the top one.

unaware	unhealthy	unequal	unlikely	unsafe	uncertain
unawere	(unhealthy)	unegual	nulikely	unsefe	(uncertain)
unavare	nuhealthy	(unequal)	unlihely	nusafe	nucertain
(unaware)	unhaelthy	ueqaul	(unlikely)	(unsafe)	uncertian

C Fill in the boxes with the correct spelling words.

1.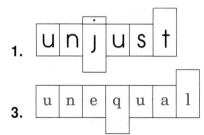

2.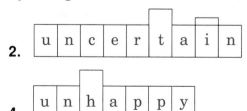

3. | u | n | e | q | u | a | l |

4. | u | n | h | a | p | p | y |

Name _____

3

Lesson 1

DAY 2

Words with *un-*

unaware	unequal	unsafe	unjust
unhealthy	unlikely	unhappy	uncertain

A The prefix *un* means "not." "Unhappy" means "not happy."
Write the correct spelling word beside each clue.

uncertain	**1.**	not sure, or not decided
unhealthy	**2.**	not well, or harmful
unaware	**3.**	not informed
unlikely	**4.**	not probable
unjust	**5.**	not fair

B Find the missing letters. Then write the word.

1. <u>u</u> <u>n</u> s <u>a</u> <u>f</u> <u>e</u>   unsafe

2. u <u>n</u> <u>h</u> <u>a</u> p <u>p</u> <u>y</u>   unhappy

3. <u>u</u> n <u>j</u> <u>u</u> <u>s</u> t   unjust

C Write the spelling words in alphabetical (ABC) order.

1. unaware   2. uncertain   3. unequal

4. unhappy   5. unhealthy   6. unjust

7. unlikely   8. unsafe

D Put an *X* on the word that is <u>not</u> the same.

1.	unaware	unaware	unaware	unaware	unaware
2.	unhealthy	unhealthy	unheathly	unhealthy	unhealthy
3.	unequal	unequal	unequal	uneqaul	unequal
4.	unlikely	unlikely	unlikely	unlikely	unlikely

4

DAY
3

Words with *un-*

unaware	unequal	unsafe	unjust
unhealthy	unlikely	unhappy	uncertain

A Fill in each blank with a spelling word.

1. Streets are an _____unsafe_____ place for children to play.

2. When her dog ran away, she felt _____unhappy_____.

3. He felt _____uncertain_____ about which show to watch.

4. She thought the umpire's ruling was _____unjust_____.

5. After we made a home run, it was _____unlikely_____ our team would lose.

6. The classes were _____unequal_____ in size.

7. Too much sugar is _____unhealthy_____ for your body.

8. The runner was _____unaware_____ that he had set a new record.

B Fill in each blank with the correct word. (The prefix *un* means "not.")

1. "Unsafe" means "not _____safe_____."

2. "Unequal" means "not _____equal_____."

3. "Unhappy" means "_____not_____ happy."

4. "Unhealthy" means "not _____healthy_____."

5. "Unlikely" means "_____not_____ _____likely_____."

6. "Uncertain" means "_____not_____ _____certain_____."

7. The word that means "not just" is _____unjust_____.

8. The word that means "not able" is _____unable_____.

9. The word that means "not paid" is _____unpaid_____.

Name _____

Words with *un-*

unaware	unequal	unsafe	unjust
unhealthy	unlikely	unhappy	uncertain

A Find each hidden word from the list.

unaware	unsafe	unkind	unclear
unhealthy	unhappy	unpaid	unborn
unequal	unjust	unreserved	unswept
unlikely	uncertain	unheard	

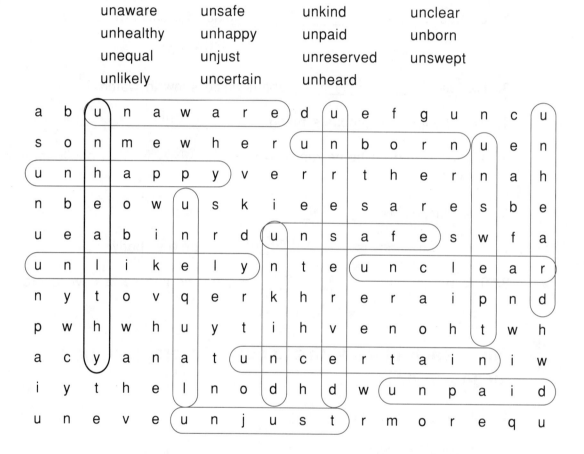

B Use the correct spelling words to complete the story.

Some people think it's a lot of trouble to buy and fix healthy foods. They

are _____unaware_____ of how simple it is to make tasty, wholesome meals

and snacks. What could be simpler than a fresh, ripe peach for dessert?

If we eat foods that are good for us, it's _____unlikely_____ we'll need

to take vitamins. A balanced diet supplies all the vitamins that a healthy

person needs.

Lesson 2 Words with *non-*

nonstop	nonsmoking	nonfat	nonfiction
nonsense	nonstick	nonliving	nonbreakable

A Fill in each blank with a spelling word. (The prefix *non* means "not.")

1. This plastic bottle is _____nonbreakable_____.

2. He only likes to drink _____nonfat_____ milk.

3. Plants are living things, and rocks are _____nonliving_____ things.

4. We flew _____nonstop_____ from New York to Chicago.

5. We sat in the _____nonsmoking_____ section of the restaurant.

6. Science books were her favorite _____nonfiction_____ books.

7. The dishes were easy to wash because of the _____nonstick_____ pots and pans.

8. Most words said backward sound like _____nonsense_____.

B Put an *X* on the word that is <u>not</u> the same.

1. nonstick	nonstick	nonstick	non~~s~~tiak	nonstick
2. nonsmoking	nonsmoking	nons~~m~~oking	nonsmoking	nonsmoking
3. nonsense	nonsense	nonsense	nonsense	nom~~s~~ense
4. nonliving	nonl~~i~~ving	nonliving	nonliving	nonliving
5. nonfiction	nonfiction	nonfiction	nonf~~i~~ctoin	nonfiction

C Fill in each blank with the correct word. (The prefix *non* means "not.")

1. "Nonliving" means "not ____living____."

2. "Nonbreakable" means "__not__ breakable."

Name _____

7

Lesson 2 — Words with *non-*

DAY 2

| nonstop | nonsmoking | nonfat | nonfiction |
| nonsense | nonstick | nonliving | nonbreakable |

A Fill in the boxes with the correct spelling words.

1. | n | o | n | s | e | n | s | e |

2. | n | o | n | l | i | v | i | n | g |

3. | n | o | n | f | i | c | t | i | o | n |

4. | n | o | n | s | t | o | p |

5. | n | o | n | s | t | i | c | k |

6. | n | o | n | f | a | t |

B Fill in each blank with a spelling word.

1. She worked _____nonstop_____ from noon until midnight.

2. That story was total _____nonsense_____.

3. This is one of the most popular _____nonfiction_____ books in years.

C Answer the questions with spelling words.

1. Which words end with *ing*?

   _____nonsmoking_____   _____nonliving_____

2. Which word has four syllables? _____nonbreakable_____

D Write the spelling words in alphabetical order.

1. _____nonbreakable_____   2. _____nonfat_____   3. _____nonfiction_____

4. _____nonliving_____   5. _____nonsense_____   6. _____nonsmoking_____

7. _____nonstick_____   8. _____nonstop_____

8

Words with *non-*

nonstop	nonsmoking	nonfat	nonfiction
nonsense	nonstick	nonliving	nonbreakable

A Circle the word that is the same as the top one.

nonsense	nonsmoking	nonstick	nonliving	nonfiction	nonbreakable
nomsense	(nonsmoking)	nonstiek	nonlivimg	nonfietion	nonbreakalbe
nonsenes	nonsnoking	(nonstick)	nomliving	(nonfiction)	(nonbreakable)
(nonsense)	nonsmohing	nonsfick	(nonliving)	nonfictoin	nondreakable

B Use the correct spelling words to complete the story.

I love to fly in airplanes. You can travel fast and meet new people.

Last week I took a _____ nonstop _____ flight to Boston. I sat

in the front section. I was next to two women. They were scientists on

their way to a meeting in Boston.

They talked to me about their work. They want to help make Earth a

clean and safe place to live. They were worried about things such as the

_____ nonbreakable _____, plastic containers we use and throw away. They

said it was important to recycle as much as we could.

"It's _____ nonsense _____ to think the problems will go away by

themselves," said one of the women. "We all need to be involved."

C Write the spelling word that comes from each root word.

break	nonbreakable	smoke	nonsmoking
live	nonliving	stop	nonstop
sense	nonsense	stick	nonstick

Name _____

9

Words with *non-*

nonstop	nonsmoking	nonfat	nonfiction
nonsense	nonstick	nonliving	nonbreakable

A Find the missing letters. Then write the word.

1. n o n l i v i n g   nonliving

2. n o n s e n s e   nonsense

3. n o n s t i c k   nonstick

4. n o n f a t   nonfat

B Where would you see these words? Match each spelling word with a place where the word might appear.

  d   **1.** nonstop   **a.** on a milk carton

  e   **2.** nonsmoking   **b.** on a plastic bottle

  a   **3.** nonfat   **c.** at a library

  c   **4.** nonfiction   **d.** on an airline schedule

  b   **5.** nonbreakable   **e.** in a special area of a restaurant

C Circle the prefix in each spelling word.

(non)stop   (non)sense   (non)smoking   (non)stick

(non)fat   (non)living   (non)fiction   (non)breakable

D Fill in each blank with the correct word.

1. The prefix *un* means "_not_."

2. The prefix *non* means "_not_."

3. "Nonstop" means "_not_ stopping."

4. "Nonsense" means "_not_ making sense."

Words with *pre-*

preview	pretest	preschool	prepaid
precook	prepare	preheat	prevent

A **Fill in each blank with the correct word. (The prefix *pre* means "at an earlier time" or "before.")**

1. "Prepaid" means "paid for at an _____earlier_____ time."

2. "Preheat" means "to _____heat_____ at an earlier time."

3. "Preview" means "to view or look at _____before_____."

B **Fill in each blank with a spelling word.**

1. Their daughter attends _____preschool_____ classes twice a week.

2. Did you _____preheat_____ the oven to 300 degrees?

3. To _____precook_____ food means to cook it just a little.

4. Before using the workbook, she took the _____pretest_____.

5. We saw the _____preview_____ for the new adventure movie.

6. She will _____prepare_____ for the race by running three miles every day.

7. The rain did not _____prevent_____ him from leaving.

8. The hotel bill was _____prepaid_____ by the company.

C **Circle the word that is the same as the top one.**

preview	pretest	prepare	preschool	prepaid	prevent
prewiew	pretets	(prepare)	perschool	prepiad	prevemt
perview	pertest	perpare	presckool	prepaib	pervent
previeiw	(pretest)	preprae	(preschool)	predaip	(prevent)
(preview)	prestet	brepare	preschol	(prepaid)	prenevt

Name _____

Words with *pre-*

DAY 2

preview	pretest	preschool	prepaid
precook	prepare	preheat	prevent

A Use the correct spelling words to complete the story.

My brother cooks great pizza. It's fun to watch him. He acts like the world's greatest chef. I'm going to take my video camera to his house tonight and tape him making one of his pizzas.

We planned the taping step by step. First, my brother will _____preheat_____ the oven. Then he'll _____precook_____ a tomato sauce and spread it on the dough. After that, he'll add cheese and other ingredients. He'll bake the pizza for ten minutes.

After he makes the pizza, our only problem will be what to _____preview_____ first, the tape or the pizza.

B Fill in each blank with a spelling word.

1. Write the words that end with the consonant *t*.

   _____preheat_____   _____pretest_____   _____prevent_____

2. Write the words that you might find in a recipe.

   _____precook_____   _____preheat_____   _____prepare_____

3. To stop something before it happens is to _____prevent_____ it.

4. To _____preview_____ means "to look at an earlier time."

C Write the correct spelling word beside each clue.

_____preschool_____   **1.** school attended before elementary school

_____pretest_____   **2.** to test before

DAY 3

Words with *pre-*

preview	pretest	preschool	prepaid
precook	prepare	preheat	prevent

A Put an *X* on the word that is <u>not</u> the same.

1. preview	preview	preview	pre~~v~~eiw	preview
2. prevent	prevent	per~~v~~ent	prevent	prevent
3. precook	pre~~c~~ool	precook	precook	precook
4. pretest	pretest	pretest	pretest	pre~~s~~tet
5. prepare	prepare	prep~~e~~re	prepare	prepare
6. preheat	preheat	preheat	pre~~h~~aet	preheat
7. prepaid	prep~~a~~ird	prepaid	prepaid	prepaid
8. preschool	preschool	pres~~c~~kool	preschool	preschool

B Write the spelling words in alphabetical order.

1. ____precook____ 2. ____preheat____ 3. ____prepaid____

4. ____prepare____ 5. ____preschool____ 6. ____pretest____

7. ____prevent____ 8. ____preview____

C Circle the prefix in each spelling word.

(pre)view   (pre)test   (pre)school   (pre)pare

(pre)cook   (pre)paid   (pre)heat   (pre)vent

D Find the missing letters. Then write the word.

1. __p__ __r__ __e__ __v__ __i__ __e__ w   ____preview____

2. __p__ __r__ __e__ h __e__ __a__ __t__   ____preheat____

Name _____

Words with *pre-*

preview	pretest	preschool	prepaid
precook	prepare	preheat	prevent

A Use spelling words to complete the puzzle.

Across

2. to fix or get ready for

5. to keep from happening

6. nursery school

Down

1. to test before

3. to look at before

4. to cook at an earlier time

Note: Annotated answers are provided only for exercises which require students to choose among answers.

Across: 2. prepare 5. prevent 6. preschool
Down: 1. pretest 3. preview 4. precook

B Complete each sentence.

1. I will prepare _____.

2. I can prevent _____.

3. The preschool _____.

4. We saw a preview of _____.

5. She has prepaid _____.

14

Lesson 4

DAY 1

Homonyms

peace	some	bow	waist
piece	sum	bough	waste

A Fill in each blank with a spelling word.

1. The two countries ended the war by signing a ___peace___ treaty.

2. For the ___sum___ of ten dollars, you can buy the shirt.

3. The pants were too large at the ___waist___.

4. ___Some___ of the students are having a bake sale to raise money.

5. I like to sit on a ___bough___ of a tree.

6. At the end of the play, she came out to take a ___bow___.

7. We have to be careful not to ___waste___ our water.

8. He cut the large ___piece___ of paper in half.

B Circle the word that is the same as the top one.

piece	peace	some	bough	waste	waist
peice	(peace)	sone	dough	waist	wasit
biece	paece	same	(bough)	wasfe	waisl
(piece)	peaec	soem	baugh	vaste	waste
pieec	deace	(some)	bougk	(waste)	woist
pieoe	peoce	osme	bongh	woste	(waist)

C Write a spelling word under each picture.

1. ___bow___

2. ___waist___

3. ___bough___

Name _____

15

Homonyms

peace	some	bow	waist
piece	sum	bough	waste

A **Use the correct spelling words to complete the story.**

My family likes to water-ski. Last week, we took ____some____ friends

with us to ski at the lake. My sister wanted to ski first.

She put a life preserver around her ____waist____ and jumped in the

lake. The boat pulled her up and she was off. Our friends cheered from the

boat when she did some of her tricks. But when my sister tried to take a

____bow____, she tumbled into the water. Luckily, she wasn't hurt.

B **Put an X on the word that is not the same.**

1. piece	piece	piece	pei̶c̶e	piece
2. peace	pea̶e̶c	peace	peace	peace
3. some	some	some	some	sa̶m̶e
4. sum	su̶n	sum	sum	sum
5. bow	bow	bow	bow	do̶w
6. bough	bough	bo̶u̶gh	bough	bough

C **Fill in each blank with the correct word.**

1. "Waist" and ____waste____ are homonyms.

2. "Bow" and "bough" are ____homonyms____.

3. "Peace" and ____piece____ are homonyms.

4. "Some" and ____sum____ are ____homonyms____.

Homonyms

peace	some	bow	waist
piece	sum	bough	waste

A Find each hidden word from the list.

piece	niece	peace	waist
waste	paste	taste	baste
hum	glum	plum	sum
gum	some	come	bough
dough	row	bow	sow
mow			

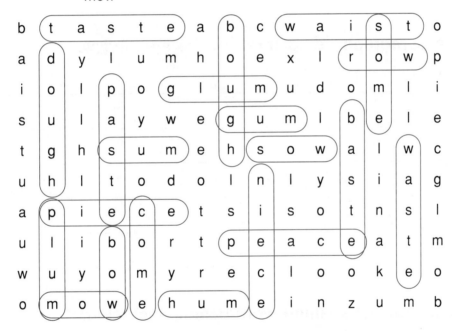

B Below are guide words. Write the spelling word that would come between each pair in the dictionary.

<u> waist </u> **1.** wage—wait

<u> sum </u> **2.** stump—swim

<u> piece </u> **3.** pet—pony

<u> bough </u> **4.** boat—bought

<u> peace </u> **5.** pace—peat

Name _____

Lesson 4   Homonyms

DAY 4

peace	some	bow	waist
piece	sum	bough	waste

A Find the missing letters. Then write the word.

1. p e a c e   _____peace_____

2. s o m e   _____some_____

3. p i e c e   _____piece_____

4. w a s t e   _____waste_____

B Write a paragraph using three of the spelling words.

_____

_____

_____

_____

_____

_____

C Write the correct spelling word beside each clue.

_____piece_____   **1.** a part separated from a whole

_____waist_____   **2.** found midway between knee and shoulder

_____waste_____   **3.** garbage, or careless use

_____peace_____   **4.** opposite of war

_____bough_____   **5.** branch of a tree

_____sum_____   **6.** whole amount

_____bow_____   **7.** front of a boat, or to bend at the waist

DAY 1

Words with *dis-*

dislike	disagree	discount	disinfect
disappear	dishonest	disconnect	disorganize

A Fill in each blank with a spelling word. (The prefix *dis* can mean "to undo.")

1. The store offered a _____discount_____ on the sweaters after winter.

2. Do you _____dislike_____ spinach?

3. You need to clean a wound to _____disinfect_____ it.

4. My friend and I sometimes _____disagree_____ on which shows to see.

5. The magician will make the coin _____disappear_____.

6. Stealing is _____dishonest_____.

7. His loud remarks were meant to _____disorganize_____ the meeting.

8. Please _____disconnect_____ the cord before repairing the lamp.

B Fill in the boxes with the correct spelling words.

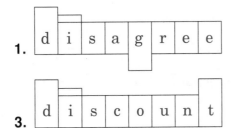

1. | d | i | s | a | g | r | e | e |

2. | d | i | s | h | o | n | e | s | t |

3. | d | i | s | c | o | u | n | t |

4. | d | i | s | i | n | f | e | c | t |

C Circle the word that is the same as the top one.

disappear	dishonest	discount	disconnect	disorganize
disapear	(dishonest)	biscount	disconect	(disorganize)
(disappear)	dishanest	disconut	(disconnect)	disroganize
bisappear	dishonset	(discount)	bisconnect	disorgamize

Name _____

Lesson 5

Words with *dis-*

dislike	disagree	discount	disinfect
disappear	dishonest	disconnect	disorganize

A **Write the spelling words in alphabetical order.**

1. _____disagree_____ 2. _____disappear_____ 3. _____disconnect_____

4. _____discount_____ 5. _____dishonest_____ 6. _____disinfect_____

7. _____dislike_____ 8. _____disorganize_____

B **Circle the prefix in each spelling word.**

(dis)like   (dis)appear   (dis)agree   (dis)honest

(dis)count   (dis)connect   (dis)infect   (dis)organize

C **Write the correct spelling word beside each clue.**

_____discount_____   **1.** to subtract from a price

_____disconnect_____   **2.** to separate one part from another

_____disappear_____   **3.** to pass out of sight

_____disorganize_____   **4.** to destroy the order of something

_____disagree_____   **5.** to have a different opinion

_____disinfect_____   **6.** to clean

_____dishonest_____   **7.** not truthful

D **Fill in each blank with a spelling word.**

1. Write the words that have two syllables.

_____discount_____   _____dislike_____

2. Write the word that has four syllables. _____disorganize_____

Words with *dis-*

dislike	disagree	discount	disinfect
disappear	dishonest	disconnect	disorganize

A **Find the missing letters. Then write the word.**

1. d i s i n f e c t   disinfect

2. d i s c o u n t   discount

3. d i s a p p e a r   disappear

4. d i s a g r e e   disagree

B **Put an *X* on the word that is not the same.**

1. dislike	dislike	dislike	disk̶ile	dislike
2. disappear	disappear	disa̶pear	disappear	disappear
3. disagree	disagree	disagree	disagree	disg̶ree
4. dishonest	dish̶anest	dishonest	dishonest	dishonest
5. discount	discount	discount	disc̶onut	discount
6. disconnect	disc̶onect	disconnect	disconnect	disconnect
7. disinfect	disinfect	disinfect	disim̶fect	disinfect

C **Use the correct spelling words to complete the story.**

I _____dislike_____ working with electricity. It can be dangerous. I try

to be careful when I work with plugs, wires, and outlets. This week, I fixed

an outlet in my house. I saved money by buying a new one at a ___discount___

hardware store. I turned off the current to my house. Then I was able to

_____disconnect_____ the outlet and replace it with the new one, without the

fear of being shocked.

Name _____

Words with *dis-*

dislike	disagree	discount	disinfect
disappear	dishonest	disconnect	disorganize

A **Find each hidden word from the list.**

dislike	disable	disown
disappear	dismiss	displace
disagree	disadvantage	disbelieve
dishonest	disarm	disapprove
discount	discolor	disloyal
disconnect	discourage	disgrace
disinfect	discriminate	distrust
disorganize	disobey	discard

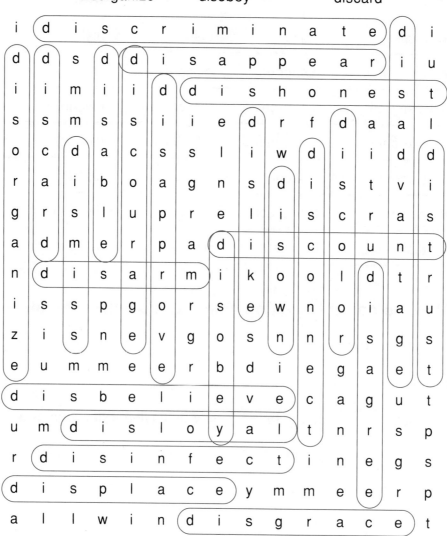

unaware	unsafe	nonstop	nonfat	preview
unhealthy	unhappy	nonsense	nonliving	precook
unequal	unjust	nonsmoking	nonfiction	pretest
unlikely	uncertain	nonstick	nonbreakable	preheat

A **Write a spelling word under each picture.**

1. _____unhappy_____ 2. _____unequal_____ 3. _____nonbreakable_____

B **Fill in each blank with a spelling word.**

1. The sky is blue, so it seems _____unlikely_____ that it will rain.

2. I had to _____preheat_____ the oven before baking the cookies.

3. He was _____uncertain_____ about his plans for the weekend.

4. Have you seen the _____preview_____ for that movie?

5. She could not understand the writing because it was _____nonsense_____ .

6. I was working inside and _____unaware_____ that it was snowing outside.

7. My family drinks _____nonfat_____ milk.

8. I love to read fiction and _____nonfiction_____ stories.

9. The hurtful comments were _____unjust_____ .

10. They will take a _____pretest_____ before they take the test.

11. I like to cook with a _____nonstick_____ frying pan.

12. It is _____unhealthy_____ to eat junk food.

Name _____

23

preschool	peace	bow	dislike	discount
prepaid	piece	bough	disappear	disconnect
prepare	some	waist	disagree	disinfect
prevent	sum	waste	dishonest	disorganize

C Find the missing letters. Then write the word.

1. s __o__ __m__ e _____ some
2. __b__ o __u__ __g__ h _____ bough
3. __d__ i __s__ l __i__ k __e___ _____ dislike
4. p __r__ __e__ s c __h__ o o l _____ preschool
5. d __i__ __s__ a __g__ re __e__ _____ disagree
6. d __i__ __s__ c __o__ n n __e__ c t _____ disconnect

D Use the correct spelling words to complete the story.

Some people like to shop for clothes, but only if they are a bargain. They

___prepare___ for shopping by looking at ads in the newspaper. They

enjoy finding a ___discount___ on the price of an item.

For serious shoppers, it is important to buy a quality product. They don't want

to ___waste___ their money on something that won't last very long. To

___prevent___ this from happening, they look carefully at each

___piece___ of clothing they would like to buy. The clothing must be well

made. For example, if a shirt has a button on it, the button should not be hanging

by a thread. It should be sewn on tightly. Also, a pair of pants should fit in the

___waist___ and the hips.

Lesson 6

DAY 1

Words with *sub-*

subway	subfreezing	submarine	subsoil
subzero	suburban	subtitle	submerge

A **Fill in each blank with a spelling word. (The prefix *sub* can mean "under" or "beneath.")**

1. The _____ subsoil _____ was mostly made of clay.

2. Our temperature often dips below freezing, and sometimes we have _____ subzero _____ weather.

3. The _____ submarine _____ slid below the water's surface.

4. The movie has a short main title and a long _____ subtitle _____.

5. Southern Florida rarely has _____ subfreezing _____ weather.

6. We rode the _____ subway _____ in Boston.

7. The _____ suburban _____ house looked like many others around it.

8. The boy liked to _____ submerge _____ his toys in the pool.

B **Fill in the boxes with the correct spelling words.**

1. | s | u | b | s | o | i | l |

2. | s | u | b | t | i | t | l | e |

3. | s | u | b | z | e | r | o |

4. | s | u | b | m | a | r | i | n | e |

5. | s | u | b | u | r | b | a | n |

6. | s | u | b | f | r | e | e | z | i | n | g |

C **Circle the prefix in each spelling word.**

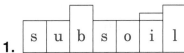 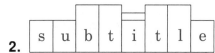
(sub)way   (sub)zero   (sub)freezing   (sub)urban

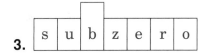 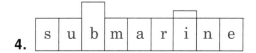
(sub)marine   (sub)title   (sub)soil   (sub)merge

Name _____

25

DAY 2

Words with *sub-*

subway	subfreezing	submarine	subsoil
subzero	suburban	subtitle	submerge

A Fill in each blank with the right word. (The prefix *sub* can mean "under" or "beneath.")

1. "Subfreezing" means "___beneath, under___ freezing temperatures."

2. A "subtitle" is a title ___beneath, under___ the main title.

3. "Subsoil" is soil ___beneath, under___ the surface soil.

4. A "subway" is a railroad that is ___beneath, under___ the ground.

B Write a spelling word under each picture.

1. ___submarine___

2. ___subway___

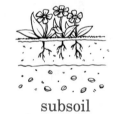

3. ___subsoil___

C Circle the word that is the same as the top one.

suburban	submarine	subtitle	subsoil	submerge
sudurban	submanire	sudtitle	(subsoil)	sudmerge
subabrun	submarime	(subtitle)	sudsoil	submenge
(suburban)	(submarine)	subtilte	subsiol	subnerge
suburdan	sudmarine	snbtitle	subsoit	(submerge)

D Write the spelling words in alphabetical order.

1. ___subfreezing___   2. ___submarine___   3. ___submerge___

4. ___subsoil___   5. ___subtitle___   6. ___suburban___

7. ___subway___   8. ___subzero___

Words with *sub-*

| subway | subfreezing | submarine | subsoil |
| subzero | suburban | subtitle | submerge |

A Write the correct spelling word beside each clue.

_____subsoil_____ **1.** earth that is beneath the surface

_____submerge_____ **2.** to put something under water

_____subway_____ **3.** a railroad underground

_____subfreezing_____ **4.** below 32 degrees F

_____suburban_____ **5.** having to do with an area close to a city

_____submarine_____ **6.** an underwater ship

B Use each spelling word in a sentence.

subway _____

suburban _____

submerge _____

submarine _____

C Put an *X* on the word that is <u>not</u> the same.

1. subway	subway	subway	su~~dw~~ay	subway
2. subzero	sub~~z~~eno	subzero	subzero	subzero
3. suburban	suburban	subu~~r~~dan	suburban	suburban
4. submarine	subm~~a~~nire	submarine	submarine	submarine
5. subtitle	subtitle	sub~~ti~~te	subtitle	subtitle
6. subsoil	subsoil	subsoil	subsoil	sub~~s~~iol
7. submerge	submerge	submerge	sud~~m~~erge	submerge

Name _____

Lesson 6   Words with *sub-*

DAY 4

subway	subfreezing	submarine	subsoil
subzero	suburban	subtitle	submerge

A **Use the correct spelling words to complete the story.**

Last night was the coldest it had been all winter. The weather forecast was

for temperatures well below freezing. We seldom have _____subfreezing_____

weather where we live. I made sure we had plenty of wood for the fireplace.

We brought our cats indoors.

Our house is in a _____suburban_____ part of town. It was much colder

out here than we thought it would be. It got down to two degrees below zero.

This is the first time we've had _____subzero_____ temperatures.

B **Fill in each blank with a spelling word.**

1. Write the words that have two syllables.

_____submerge_____   _____subway_____   _____subsoil_____

2. Write the words that have a long *e* sound.

_____subfreezing_____   _____subzero_____   _____submarine_____

3. Write the three-syllable word whose accent is on the last syllable.

_____submarine_____

C **Find the missing letters. Then write the word.**

1. s _u_ b _u_ r b _a_ n _____suburban_____

2. _s_ _u_ b w _a_ _y_ _____subway_____

3. _s_ _u_ b m _e_ r g _e_ _____submerge_____

Words with *re-*

refill	review	repair	reclaim
recycle	refund	recharge	rewind

A **Fill in each blank with a spelling word. (The prefix *re* means "to do again.")**

1. You can _____recycle_____ glass and newspapers, instead of throwing them away.

2. The company will _____refund_____ my money if I'm not pleased.

3. She had to _____recharge_____ the car's battery.

4. The country will _____reclaim_____ its wetlands for use as farms.

5. My running shoes are in need of _____repair_____.

6. Will you please _____refill_____ my cup with coffee?

7. Let's _____rewind_____ the tape and watch it from the beginning.

8. The class will _____review_____ Chapter 10 before the test tomorrow.

B **Circle the prefix in each spelling word.**

(re)fill   (re)cycle   (re)view   (re)fund

(re)pair   (re)charge   (re)claim   (re)wind

C **Find the missing letters. Then write the word.**

1. r e v i e w   _____review_____

2. r e f u n d   _____refund_____

D **Fill in each blank with the correct word.**

1. All of the spelling words, except one, have _____two_____ syllables.

2. The word _____recycle_____ has _____three_____ syllables.

Name _____

29

Lesson 7

Words with *re-*

refill	review	repair	reclaim
recycle	refund	recharge	rewind

A Fill in the boxes with the correct spelling words.

1.  r e v i e w

2. 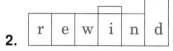 r e w i n d

3. 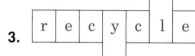 r e c y c l e

4. 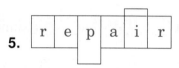 r e f u n d

5. r e p a i r

6. 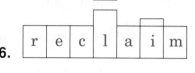 r e c l a i m

B Circle the word that is the same as the top one.

recycle	review	repair	recharge	reclaim	rewind
recyle	reveiw	repiar	reckarge	recalim	rewimd
recycel	(review)	regair	rechrage	(reclaim)	rewinb
(recycle)	rewiev	repain	recharqe	reelaim	revind
necycle	reveiv	(repair)	(recharge)	reclain	(rewind)

C Write the spelling words in alphabetical order.

1. _____recharge_____ 2. _____reclaim_____ 3. _____recycle_____

4. _____refill_____ 5. _____refund_____ 6. _____repair_____

7. _____review_____ 8. _____rewind_____

D Complete each sentence.

1. I will <u>repair</u> _____.

2. Please <u>recycle</u> _____.

3. She has a <u>refund</u> _____.

4. Did you <u>refill</u> _____?

30

Words with *re-*

refill	review	repair	reclaim
recycle	refund	recharge	rewind

A Write a paragraph using three of the spelling words.

_____

_____

_____

_____

_____

B Write the correct spelling word beside each clue.

review	**1.** to see or examine again
reclaim	**2.** to recover land
rewind	**3.** to wind something again
recharge	**4.** to restore to new, as with a battery
refill	**5.** to fill again
recycle	**6.** to treat and use again
repair	**7.** to fix a broken item
refund	**8.** money due to a person

C Fill in each blank with the correct word.

1. The prefix for all the spelling words is _____re_____.

2. The prefix _____re_____ means "to do again."

3. "Refill" means "to _____fill_____ again."

4. "Review" means "to view _____again_____."

Name _____

Words with *re-*

refill	review	repair	reclaim
recycle	refund	recharge	rewind

A Put an *X* on the word that is <u>not</u> the same.

1.	refill	refill	refill	re̶fi̶le	refill
2.	refund	refund	refu̶nb	refund	refund
3.	recycle	recy̶cel	recycle	recycle	recycle
4.	repair	repair	repair	reg̶air	repair
5.	recharge	recharge	recharge	recho̶rge	recharge
6.	rewind	rewind	rewind	rewind	reni̶wd
7.	review	reve̶iw	review	review	review
8.	reclaim	reclaim	recl̶iam	reclaim	reclaim

B Use the correct spelling words to complete the story.

Let's _____ review _____ some ways that we can take care of Earth's

land, air, and water. To keep from harming our soil and streams, we can

_____ recycle _____ much of what we use. Paper, glass, and cans can be

saved. Old batteries and motor oil are being used again.

Instead of throwing out old clothes and broken tools, we can _____ repair _____

them. Food scraps and leaves are saved as compost, which then feeds Earth.

We should think about what we do in our daily lives. It's important that we

do all we can to help our planet.

Homonyms

rain	their	haul	pair
rein	there	hall	pear

A **Fill in each blank with a spelling word.**

1. They will meet us _____there_____ tomorrow.

2. We have an apple tree and a _____pear_____ tree in our yard.

3. Will you help your brother _____haul_____ the wood?

4. I walked down the long, wide _____hall_____.

5. He lost a _____pair_____ of gloves in the park.

6. _____Their_____ house has a beautiful garden.

7. A _____rein_____ can be used to control an animal.

8. I like the sound of _____rain_____ on a rooftop.

B **Find the missing letters. Then write the word.**

1. _p_ _e_ a _r_   _____pear_____

2. _r_ a _i_ n   _____rain_____

3. _h_ a u _l_   _____haul_____

C **Fill in each blank with a spelling word.**

1. Write the word that ends with a silent *e*. _____there_____

2. Write the two words that have five letters.

 _____there_____ _____their_____

3. Write the word that ends with a double consonant. _____hall_____

4. Write the word for a fruit whose first three letters spell a vegetable.

 _____pear_____

Name _____

33

Homonyms

rain	their	haul	pair
rein	there	hall	pear

A Circle the word that is the same as the top one.

rein	their	there	haul	pair	pear
rien	thein	tlere	(haul)	pain	gear
reim	thier	(there)	hual	(pair)	pean
neir	(their)	theer	kaul	piar	(pear)
(rein)	there	htere	haut	gair	paer

B Use the correct spelling words to complete the letter.

Dear Brenda,

I'm having a great time at camp. _____There_____ is a lot to do. We hike,

canoe, and learn crafts. I'm making a _____pair_____ of earrings. We eat in a

big dining _____hall_____. We haven't had any _____rain_____, so I've been

swimming every day. I wish you were here to share the fun.

Your friend,

Michelle

C Write the spelling words in alphabetical order.

1. _____hall_____ 2. _____haul_____ 3. _____pair_____ 4. _____pear_____

5. _____rain_____ 6. _____rein_____ 7. _____their_____ 8. _____there_____

D Write the spelling words that rhyme with the word pair.

1. main   train   pain   _____rein, rain_____

2. tall   ball   fall   _____haul, hall_____

Lesson 8   Homonyms

rain	their	haul	pair
rein	there	hall	pear

A Write the correct spelling word beside each clue.

1. something to eat _____ pear

2. an element of weather _____ rain

3. to carry _____ haul

4. a space within a building _____ hall

5. two similar items _____ pair

6. belonging to them _____ their

B Put an *X* on the word that is <u>not</u> the same.

1.	their	~~thier~~	their	their	their
2.	haul	haul	haul	haul	~~hual~~
3.	pair	~~pain~~	pair	pair	pair
4.	there	there	there	~~theer~~	there

C Write a spelling word under each picture.

1. _____ rein

2. _____ rain

3. _____ hall

4. _____ haul

5. _____ pair

6. _____ pear

Name _____

Homonyms

rain	their	haul	pair
rein	there	hall	pear

A Use each spelling word in a sentence.

rein _____

their _____

there _____

haul _____

pair _____

pear _____

hall _____

B Find each hidden word from the list.

rain	gain	main	pain
rein	their	there	haul
hall	ball	tall	mall
pair	chair	stairs	hair
pear	bear	wear	homonym

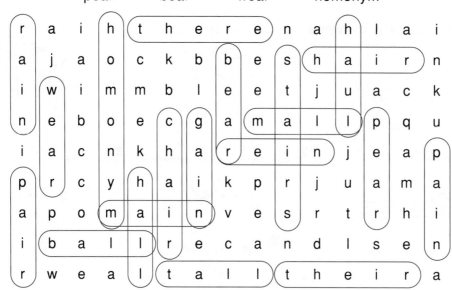

DAY
1

Words with *mis-*

misplace	mislead	mistreat	misfortune
misprint	misbehave	misuse	misunderstand

A **Fill in each blank with a spelling word. (The prefix *mis* can mean "lack of" or "error in.")**

1. I hope I didn't _____misunderstand_____ your message.

2. Information that's untrue can be used to deceive or _____mislead_____ people.

3. The newspaper article contained a _____misprint_____.

4. To _____mistreat_____ an animal is cruel and unkind.

5. The young boy promised not to _____misbehave_____ while his parents were away.

6. _____Misfortune_____ happened to the boy when he acted unkind.

7. We should not _____misuse_____ our natural resources.

8. Did you _____misplace_____ your necklace?

B **Fill in the boxes with the correct spelling words.**

1. | m | i | s | u | s | e |

2. | m | i | s | p | r | i | n | t |

3. | m | i | s | p | l | a | c | e |

4. | m | i | s | f | o | r | t | u | n | e |

C **Circle the prefix in each spelling word.**

(mis)place   (mis)print   (mis)lead   (mis)understand

(mis)treat   (mis)use   (mis)fortune   (mis)behave

Name _____

37

DAY 2

Words with *mis-*

| misplace | mislead | mistreat | misfortune |
| misprint | misbehave | misuse | misunderstand |

A Fill in each blank with a spelling word. (The prefix *mis* can mean "bad" and "badly," or "wrong" and "wrongly.")

1. Something _____wrongly_____ printed is a misprint.

2. "Misbehave" means "to behave _____badly_____."

3. "Mistreat" means "to treat _____badly_____."

4. "Misfortune" means "to have _____bad_____ fortune."

5. To understand wrongly is to _____misunderstand_____.

B Find the missing letters. Then write the word.

1. m i s l e a d _____mislead_____

2. m i s u s e _____misuse_____

3. m i s p l a c e _____misplace_____

C Write the spelling words in alphabetical order.

1. _____misbehave_____ 2. _____misfortune_____ 3. _____mislead_____

4. _____misplace_____ 5. _____misprint_____ 6. _____mistreat_____

7. _____misunderstand_____ 8. _____misuse_____

D Fill in each blank with a spelling word.

1. Write the two words that have three syllables.

   _____misfortune_____ _____misbehave_____

2. Write the word that has four syllables. _____misunderstand_____

Lesson 9

Words with *mis-*

| misplace | mislead | mistreat | misfortune |
| misprint | misbehave | misuse | misunderstand |

A Put an *X* on the word that is <u>not</u> the same.

1. misplace	misplace	misplace	mispalce
2. misprint	mispirnt	misprint	misprint
3. mislead	mislead	mislaed	mislead
4. mistreat	mistreat	mistreat	mistneat
5. misuse	misuse	misnse	misuse
6. misbehave	misbehave	misbehave	misdehave
7. misfortune	mistortune	misfortune	misfortune

B Use each spelling word in a sentence.

misprint _____

mistreat _____

misunderstand _____

misplace _____

misuse _____

C Circle the word that is the same as the top one.

misplace	misprint	mislead	mistreat	misuse
mispalce	misprimt	(mislead)	misterat	misues
nisplace	misprinl	mislaed	(mistreat)	nisuse
misplaec	(misprint)	mistead	mislreat	msiuse
(misplace)	misgrint	nislead	mistraet	(misuse)

Name _____

39

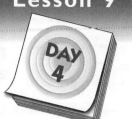 **Words with *mis-***

misplace	mislead	mistreat	misfortune
misprint	misbehave	misuse	misunderstand

A Circle the root word in each spelling word.

mis(place)   mis(print)   mis(understand)   mis(lead)

mis(treat)   mis(use)   mis(fortune)   mis(behave)

B Use the correct spelling words to complete the story.

Newspaper reporters have to use care when they write stories. They

must write the facts. They can't write their opinions. And they must try not to

_____mislead_____ readers.

Mistakes can happen in many different ways. Reporters might

_____misunderstand_____ someone they interview and write the story wrong.

When the story goes to press, there could be a _____misprint_____ in

the final copy. This could change the whole meaning of the piece. It's easy

to see why being a reporter is one of the hardest jobs.

C Fill in each blank with a spelling word.

1. Write the shortest and longest words.

_____misuse_____   _____misunderstand_____

2. Write the words that end with the letter *t*.

_____misprint_____   _____mistreat_____

3. Write the words with the long *a* sound.

_____misbehave_____   _____misplace_____

Words with *con-*

contract	congregate	conform	consent
concert	concern	confide	conduct

A Fill in each blank with a spelling word.

1. She will _____consent_____ to be president of the club.

2. A group will _____congregate_____ in the band room to practice for the parade.

3. As president, she will _____conduct_____ the meeting tonight.

4. We wrote a business agreement that's called a _____contract_____.

5. Best friends often _____confide_____ in each other.

6. My main _____concern_____ is for the health of the children.

7. Shoes will _____conform_____ to the shape of your foot.

8. We attended the band _____concert_____ last week.

B Find the missing letters. Then write the word.

1. _c_ _o_ n d _u_ _c_ _t_ _____conduct_____

2. _c_ _o_ n t _r_ _a_ c t _____contract_____

3. c _o_ _n_ s _e_ _n_ _t_ _____consent_____

4. _c_ _o_ _n_ _c_ _e_ _r_ n _____concern_____

C Write the spelling words in alphabetical order.

1. _____concern_____   2. _____concert_____   3. _____conduct_____

4. _____confide_____   5. _____conform_____   6. _____congregate_____

7. _____consent_____   8. _____contract_____

Name _____

Words with *con-*

contract	congregate	conform	consent
concert	concern	confide	conduct

A Circle the root word in each spelling word.

(contract)ion   (congregate)d   (conform)able   (consent)ing

(concert)s   (concern)ing   (confide)d   (conduct)ion

B Write the correct spelling word beside each clue.

1. _____consent_____ to agree to something

2. _____concert_____ a musical program

3. _____congregate_____ to get together

4. _____confide_____ to share a secret

C Circle the word that is the same as the top one.

contract	concert	conduct	conform	confide	consent
contarct	concent	conduet	confrom	confied	(consent)
(contract)	comcert	conbuct	conforn	(confide)	cansent
conlract	(concert)	comduct	(conform)	canfide	cansemt
controct	concret	(conduct)	contorm	confibe	consnet

D Fill in each blank with the correct word.

1. How many spelling words have two syllables? _____seven_____

2. Which spelling word has three syllables? _____congregate_____

3. Which spelling words end with a silent *e*?

_____confide_____ . _____congregate_____

Words with *con-*

contract	congregate	conform	consent
concert	concern	confide	conduct

A Use each spelling word in a sentence.

confide _____

contract _____

concern _____

conform _____

concert _____

B Fill in the boxes with the correct spelling words.

1. c o n f o r m

2. c o n t r a c t

3. c o n d u c t

4. c o n g r e g a t e

5. c o n c e r n

6. c o n f i d e

C Put an *X* on the word that is <u>not</u> the same.

1. contract	contract	contract	cont~~a~~rct	contract
2. conduct	conduct	conduct	conduct	com~~d~~uct
3. consent	consent	con~~s~~ant	consent	consent
4. concert	con~~c~~ret	concert	concert	concert
5. congregate	congregate	congregate	congregate	conge~~r~~gate

Name _____

Words with *con-*

contract	congregate	conform	consent
concert	concern	confide	conduct

A Write the correct spelling word beside each clue.

_____contract_____   **1.** agreement

_____conform_____   **2.** to come to have the same form

_____conduct_____   **3.** to lead

_____concern_____   **4.** worry

B Below are guide words. Write the spelling words that would come between each pair in the dictionary.

_____concern_____   _____concert_____   **1.** concede—condor

_____consent_____   _____contract_____   **2.** connection—contraction

_____conduct_____   _____confide_____   **3.** concussion—confirm

_____conform_____   _____congregate_____   **4.** conflict—connect

C Use the correct spelling words to complete the story.

Each spring, the people here _____conduct_____ a "trash day." This

is when we clean up our town.

Early in the morning, grownups and kids _____congregate_____ with

trash bags in hand. We pick up litter thrown along the roads. We find glass

bottles, cans, food wrappers, and all kinds of things.

After all the trash is gathered, we sort it for things to recycle. Then we

have a big picnic in the park. It's nice to live in a town where people have

_____concern_____ for keeping the roadways clean.

subway	subfreezing	refill	recycle	rain
subzero	suburban	review	recharge	rein
subsoil	submarine	refund	reclaim	hall
subtitle	submerge	rewind	repair	haul

A Write a spelling word under each picture.

1. _____subway_____   2. _____submarine_____   3. _____rain_____

B Fill in each blank with a spelling word.

1. They were going to _____haul_____ their trash to the recycling center.

2. The _____subzero_____ weather kept the car from starting.

3. She lives in a _____suburban_____ area outside of the city.

4. You will need to _____rewind_____ that old clock several times a day.

5. You can _____recharge_____ those batteries instead of buying new ones.

6. We will _____repair_____ that broken sink today.

7. It is important to _____recycle_____ paper, glass, and plastic.

8. The room is at the end of the long, narrow _____hall_____.

9. Please _____refill_____ the pitcher of water when it is empty.

10. The soil beneath the surface soil is called _____subsoil_____.

11. When I returned the shirt, the cashier gave me a _____refund_____.

12. Can you tell me the _____subtitle_____ of that movie?

Name _____

misprint	misplace	contract	concert	pair
mislead	misbehave	congregate	concern	pear
mistreat	misfortune	conform	confide	there
misuse	misunderstand	conduct	consent	their

C **Find the missing letters. Then write the word.**

1. p __a__ i __r__   pair

2. __c__ __o__ __n__ f i __d__ e   confide

3. c __o__ n __f__ __o__ __r__ m   conform

4. __m__ __i__ s __t__ r e __a__ t   mistreat

5. m i __s__ p __l__ __a__ __c__ e   misplace

6. c __o__ n __s__ __e__ n __t__   consent

D **Use the correct spelling words to complete the story.**

    A good friend is someone who is always there for you. A friend shares your life and is honest with you. A good friend will never ___mislead___ you. It is as though there is an unspoken agreement or ___contract___ for trusting each other. If you are unlucky or have a ___misfortune___, you can count on a good friend to show ___concern___ for you.

    Your way of behaving or ___conduct___ is important, too. You should always be ___there___ for your friend as well. When a friend wants to tell you a secret or ___confide___ in you, you must keep that information to yourself. It is important for a friend to know that you can always be trusted. A good friendship is priceless!

Words with *de-*

descend	deposit	decrease	depart
dehydrate	decide	deflate	deliver

A Fill in each blank with a spelling word. (The prefix *de* can mean "to remove," "to undo," or "to reduce.")

1. We had to _____descend_____ a stairway to get to the subway station.

2. The florist will _____deliver_____ the flowers today.

3. Did you _____deposit_____ your check last Friday?

4. The train will _____depart_____ for Washington at noon.

5. When you dry something, you _____dehydrate_____ it.

6. He could not _____decide_____ where to go for his vacation.

7. You can _____deflate_____ the tire by pressing the stem.

8. The hot water will cause the shirt to _____decrease_____ in size.

B Fill in each blank with a spelling word.

1. Which words have three syllables?

_____dehydrate_____ _____deposit_____ _____deliver_____

2. Which words have a long *i* sound?

_____decide_____ _____dehydrate_____

3. Which word contains three *e*'s? _____decrease_____

C Write a spelling word under each picture.

1. _____deliver_____ 2. _____descend_____ 3. _____deposit_____

Name _____

47

Lesson 11

Words with *de-*

descend	deposit	decrease	depart
dehydrate	decide	deflate	deliver

A Fill in the boxes with the correct spelling words.

1. d e c r e a s e

2. d e f l a t e

3. d e p o s i t

4. d e l i v e r

5. d e p a r t

6. d e s c e n d

7. d e c i d e

8. d e h y d r a t e

B Write the spelling words in alphabetical order.

1. _____decide_____   2. _____decrease_____

3. _____deflate_____   4. _____dehydrate_____

5. _____deliver_____   6. _____depart_____

7. _____deposit_____   8. _____descend_____

C Circle the word that is the same as the top one.

descend	dehydrate	deposit	decide	depart	deliver
decsend	dehybrate	depoist	decibe	bepart	delivre
descemd	dehydarte	degosit	decidc	(depart)	beliver
descenb	behydrate	(deposit)	(decide)	depamt	deliwer
(descend)	(dehydrate)	depasit	becide	pedart	(deliver)

48

Words with *de-*

descend	deposit	decrease	depart
dehydrate	decide	deflate	deliver

A **Fill in each blank with the correct word. (The prefix *de* can mean "undo," "remove," or "reduce." To "decode" means "to undo a code." To "defog" means "to remove fog.")**

1. "Dehydrate" means "to ___remove, reduce___ the water."

2. "Deflate" means "to ___remove, reduce___ the air."

B **Which spelling word might be used in discussing each topic?**

___decrease___ 1. clothes that shrunk in the dryer

___descend___ 2. going down a rope

___decide___ 3. choosing a college

___depart___ 4. leaving

___deflate___ 5. letting air out of a bike tire

___deposit___ 6. adding money to an account

___dehydrate___ 7. drying fruit to preserve it

C **Use the correct spelling words to complete the story.**

When I was twelve, I wanted to go to summer camp. But my parents and

I couldn't ___decide___ which camp to choose.

For weeks, the mail carrier would ___deliver___ information on

camps that we had asked for. At last, we chose a camp near a lake. I could

learn to canoe and water-ski there. My parents sent the camp a

___deposit___. It was one of the best decisions we ever made.

Name _____

Words with *de-*

descend	deposit	decrease	depart
dehydrate	decide	deflate	deliver

A Find the missing letters. Then write the word.

1. d e p o s i t   deposit

2. d e p a r t   depart

3. d e s c e n d   descend

4. d e l i v e r   deliver

B Find each hidden word from the list.

descend	deceive	defend	dehydrate
deflate	debate	define	deposit
depart	decay	delight	decide
deliver	deduct	degree	delay
demand	decrease	decontrol	

```
d  e  p  d  e  h  y  d  r  a  t  e  d  e  d
e  d  e  f  i  n  e  e  m  a  t  c  h  m  e
s  e  a  k  e  m  a  z  t  c  h  d  m  a  l
c  b  d  d  k  e  d  e  p  o  s  i  t  r  i
e  a  e  e  d  e  p  a  r  t  m  e  a  k  v
n  t  f  c  e  e  m  o  d  e  c  e  i  v  e
d  e  l  i  g  h  t  m  a  m  a  u  t  c  r
h  f  a  d  r  i  n  d  e  d  u  c  t  d  m
e  a  t  e  e  c  a  t  d  h  m  t  e  a  c
a  d  e  f  e  n  d  t  e  d  e  c  a  y  h
d  e  c  o  n  t  r  o  l  e  d  d  e  p  o
e  l  i  v  e  d  e  m  a  n  d  r  a  t  s
d  e  c  r  e  a  s  e  y  h  e  i  n  t  i
```

Homonyms

throne	shone	fair	it's
thrown	shown	fare	its

A Fill in each blank with a spelling word.

1. _____It's_____ beginning to rain again.

2. The bus _____fare_____ from here to the park is fifty cents.

3. The sun _____shone_____ every day at the beach.

4. The weather changed from _____fair_____ to stormy.

5. The king sat on the _____throne_____ only for ceremonies.

6. We were _____shown_____ how to play the new game.

7. She has _____thrown_____ more no-hitters than any other pitcher.

8. My cat often licks _____its_____ fur.

B Find the missing letters. Then write the word.

1. _s_ _h_ _o_ n _e_ _____shone_____

2. s _h_ _o_ _w_ n _____shown_____

C Write a spelling word under each picture.

1. _____throne_____ 2. _____fair_____ 3. _____thrown_____

D Below is a pair of guide words. Write the spelling word that would come between the pair in the dictionary.

_____fare_____ fame—fate

Name _____

Homonyms

throne	shone	fair	it's
thrown	shown	fare	its

A Circle the root word in each spelling word.

(throw)n   (show)n   (it)s

B Use "it's" or "its" in each sentence. ("It's" is a contraction of "it is" or "it has." "Its" is the possessive form of the pronoun "it." "Its" is used to show possession or ownership.)

1. _____It's_____ time to go to the hockey game.

2. The car was old, and _____its_____ metal was rusted.

3. _____It's_____ been a great year for movies and music.

4. _____It's_____ a beautiful morning.

5. The tree had lost most of _____its_____ leaves.

6. The team won many of _____its_____ games.

7. _____It's_____ strange to have snow at this time of year.

8. Do you know if _____it's_____ too late to mail the letter?

9. Did the snake show _____its_____ fangs?

C Circle the word that is the same as the top one.

throne	thrown	shone	fare	shown
(throne)	throne	shonc	faer	(shown)
throre	thromn	(shone)	fear	shone
throen	(thrown)	shown	fane	shomn
thnone	thorwn	shore	(fare)	shawn

Homonyms

throne	shone	fair	it's
thrown	shown	fare	its

A **Use the correct spelling words to complete the story.**

There once was a story about a king who grew tired of sitting at his

___throne___ all day. He didn't think it was ___fair___ to have to

stay in the castle, while others rode through the town. He called for his coach

and driver.

"___It's___ a splendid day for a ride," said the king to the driver.

"I'll let you wear my crown if you'll let me drive the coach." So they traded

places and had a fine ride through the town.

B **Write the correct spelling word beside each clue.**

___shone___	**1.** was bright
___it's___	**2.** a contraction
___thrown___	**3.** tossed
___throne___	**4.** the official chair of a king
___its___	**5.** shows ownership
___fair___	**6.** equal
___fare___	**7.** the cost of being transported, as in a bus

C **Write the spelling words in alphabetical order.**

1. ___fair___ 2. ___fare___ 3. ___its___

4. ___it's___ 5. ___shone___ 6. ___shown___

7. ___throne___ 8. ___thrown___

Name _____

throne	shone	fair	it's
thrown	shown	fare	its

A Use each spelling word in a sentence.

it's _____

its _____

thrown _____

shone _____

fair _____

throne _____

shown _____

fare _____

B Find each hidden word from the list.

throne	shone	bone	tone
thrown	shown	grown	sown
fair	hair	chair	stair
fare	mare	stare	bare
rare	dare	hare	care

```
b  o  n  e  o  g  h  a  i  r  o  m  e  s  t
h  c  h  a  i  r  s  t  o  n  b  a  a  t  o
a  m  o  s  h  o  n  e  t  r  a  r  e  a  p
r  o  s  h  o  w  n  n  o  g  r  e  s  n  h
e  s  t  t  o  n  e  d  a  r  e  o  o  e  o
s  t  a  r  e  o  t  h  r  o  n  e  w  w  n
f  a  i  r  o  c  a  r  e  w  s  o  n  e  e
f  a  r  e  t  h  r  o  w  n  f  a  r  n  o
```

DAY 1

Words with -*less*

harmless	careless	useless	thankless
painless	hopeless	helpless	thoughtless

A Fill in each blank with a spelling word. (The suffix *less* means "lack of," "free of," "without," or "not having.")

1. He wasn't thankful to have such a _____thankless_____ task.

2. The broken ax was _____useless_____ for chopping wood.

3. The rescue team did not consider the case _____hopeless_____.

4. When she lost her compass, the hiker felt _____helpless_____.

5. The removal of the tooth was nearly _____painless_____.

6. He is never _____careless_____ with matches.

7. Her _____thoughtless_____ comment upset her friend.

8. The garter snake is _____harmless_____.

B Find the missing letters. Then write the word.

1. h o p e l e s s _____hopeless_____

2. u s e l e s s _____useless_____

3. h e l p l e s s _____helpless_____

C Circle the word that is the same as the top one.

harmless	painless	careless	thankless	thoughtless
hanmless	gainless	(careless)	thamkless	(thoughtless)
karmless	(painless)	caneless	thanhless	thuoghtless
harnless	pianless	coreless	(thankless)	thouqhtless
(harmless)	paimless	carelese	thanktess	thoughttess

Name _____

Words with -*less*

harmless	**careless**	**useless**	**thankless**
painless	**hopeless**	**helpless**	**thoughtless**

A **Use the correct spelling words to complete the story.**

Many people are afraid of spiders. But most spiders won't hurt you at all.

They're quite _____harmless_____. Some people think spiders are

_____useless_____ pests. But they eat insects that can damage plants

and vegetables. To kill every spider you see is a _____thoughtless_____

thing to do.

If you study them closely, you'll see that spiders are beautiful and

graceful creatures.

B **Fill in each blank with the correct word.**

1. "Weightless" means "not having _____weight_____."

2. "Useless" means "not having _____use_____."

3. "Blameless" means "free of _____blame_____."

4. "Painless" means "free of _____pain_____."

5. "Thankless" means "without _____thanks_____."

6. "Hopeless" means "_____without_____ hope."

7. "Thoughtless" means "without _____thought_____."

C **Write the spelling words in alphabetical order.**

1. _____careless_____ 2. _____harmless_____ 3. _____helpless_____

4. _____hopeless_____ 5. _____painless_____ 6. _____thankless_____

7. _____thoughtless_____ 8. _____useless_____

DAY 3

Words with -*less*

harmless	careless	useless	thankless
painless	hopeless	helpless	thoughtless

A Put an *X* on the word that is <u>not</u> the same.

1. helpless	helpless	helpless	helpless	hep~~l~~less
2. thankless	thankless	thankless	thankless	than~~k~~less
3. painless	painless	pai~~n~~less	painless	painless
4. car~~e~~less	careless	careless	careless	careless

B Use a spelling word to describe each noun.

1. a _____thankless_____ job (no appreciation shown)

2. a _____helpless_____ puppy (needs to be cared for)

3. a _____harmless_____ spider (can't injure people)

4. a _____painless_____ operation (doesn't hurt)

5. a _____hopeless_____ problem (seems as though it will never be solved)

6. a _____careless_____ smoker (starts a forest fire)

7. a _____thoughtless_____ act (not being kind)

C Fill in each blank with a spelling word.

1. Write the word that begins with a vowel. _____useless_____

2. Write the words that have a silent *e*.

    _____careless_____   _____useless_____   _____hopeless_____

3. Write the word with the greatest number of letters. _____thoughtless_____

4. Write the word whose root word is "thank." _____thankless_____

Name _____

Words with *-less*

harmless	careless	useless	thankless
painless	hopeless	helpless	thoughtless

A Circle the suffix in each spelling word.

harm(less)   pain(less)   care(less)   hope(less)

thank(less)   help(less)   use(less)   thought(less)

B Use spelling words to complete the puzzle.

Across

3. impossible

5. without care

6. having little or no worth, or not effective

Down

1. unkind

2. unable to manage by oneself

4. without pain

Crossword grid:

1. Down: t h o u g h t
2. Down: h e l p l e s s
3. Across: h o p e l e s s
4. Down: p a i n l e s s
5. Across: c a r e l e s s
6. Across: u s e l e s s

Words with -*ful*

thoughtful	beautiful	careful	hopeful
peaceful	harmful	truthful	thankful

A Fill in each blank with a spelling word. (The suffix *ful* means "full of" or "having the qualities of.")

1. She was _____hopeful_____ her story would win a prize.

2. My mother often tells me to be _____careful_____ when I mow the lawn.

3. His cat was a _____beautiful_____ gray Persian.

4. The ocean was calm and _____peaceful_____.

5. I'm _____thankful_____ for my family and friends.

6. How _____thoughtful_____ of you to bring me flowers!

7. Too much sun can be _____harmful_____ to a person's skin.

8. He is always _____truthful_____ about his feelings.

B Write the root word of each spelling word.

1. thoughtful _____thought_____   2. truthful _____truth_____

3. peaceful _____peace_____   4. hopeful _____hope_____

5. beautiful _____beauty_____   6. thankful _____thank_____

C Circle the word that is the same as the top one.

careful	harmful	beautiful	thoughtful	thankful
caneful	harnful	beuatiful	thougthful	thamkful
coreful	hanmful	(beautiful)	thoughful	(thankful)
(careful)	harmfut	beautyful	(thoughtful)	thanhful
carefull	(harmful)	deautiful	thonghtful	thonkful

Name _____

Words with -*ful*

thoughtful	beautiful	careful	hopeful
peaceful	harmful	truthful	thankful

A Fill in each blank with the correct word.

1. "Peaceful" means "full of ____peace____."

2. "Harmful" means "full of ____harm____."

3. "Hopeful" means "full of ____hope____."

4. "Beautiful" means "____full____ __of__ beauty."

5. "Thoughtful" means "____full____ __of__ thought."

6. "Careful" means "full __of__ ____care____."

7. "Thankful" means "____full____ __of__ ____thanks____."

8. "Truthful" means "having the qualities of ____truth____."

B Fill in the boxes with the correct spelling words.

1. p e a c e f u l

2. t h o u g h t f u l

3. t h a n k f u l

4. c a r e f u l

5. b e a u t i f u l

6. h o p e f u l

C Complete each sentence with a spelling word.

1. The opposite of careless is ____careful____.

2. The opposite of dishonest is ____truthful____.

3. The opposite of thoughtless is ____thoughtful____.

DAY 3

Words with *-ful*

thoughtful	beautiful	careful	hopeful
peaceful	harmful	truthful	thankful

A Write the spelling words in alphabetical order.

1. _beautiful_   2. _careful_   3. _harmful_

4. _hopeful_   5. _peaceful_   6. _thankful_

7. _thoughtful_   8. _truthful_

B Find the missing letters. Then write the word.

1. t r u t h f u l   _truthful_

2. t h o u g h t f u l   _thoughtful_

3. h o p e f u l   _hopeful_

4. c a r e f u l   _careful_

C Use a spelling word to describe each noun.

1. a _peaceful_ beach (when it's completely calm)

2. a _hopeful_ candidate (who thinks he can win)

3. _harmful_ sun rays (that can damage your skin)

4. a _careful_ mountain climber (who watches his step)

5. _thankful_ people (whose homes were saved from a flood)

6. a _beautiful_ sunset (that everyone stopped to admire)

D Fill in each blank with the correct word.

1. How many syllables do seven of the spelling words have? _two_

2. Which spelling word has three syllables? _beautiful_

Name _____

Words with -*ful*

thoughtful	beautiful	careful	hopeful
peaceful	harmful	truthful	thankful

A **Use each spelling word in a sentence.**

thoughtful _____

peaceful _____

harmful _____

thankful _____

truthful _____

B **Below are guide words. Write the spelling word that would come between each pair in the dictionary.**

1. _____careful_____ between—desk

2. _____hopeful_____ happy—human

3. _____peaceful_____ opened—quiet

4. _____thoughtful_____ that—thunder

C **Use the correct spelling words to complete the story.**

I love spending summer vacations at our beach house by the sea. The sunrise there is such a _____beautiful_____ sight. The bright sky and gentle breeze coax me outside.

I'm _____careful_____ not to stay in the sun too long. Its rays can be _____harmful_____ to my skin. But it's hard not to stay at the beach all day. The ocean is so calm and _____peaceful_____. When I'm at the beach, my troubles melt away.

Lesson 15

Words with -ness

slowness	coldness	fairness	blackness
sickness	darkness	kindness	loudness

A **Fill in each blank with a spelling word.**

1. The _____blackness_____ of the cat reminds me of a dark night.

2. Because of the stereo's _____loudness_____, we could not talk.

3. I could never repay your _____kindness_____.

4. He missed the game due to _____sickness_____.

5. We have to say, in all _____fairness_____, that the other team

   was good.

6. After the sun went down, _____darkness_____ fell upon the campsite.

7. The train's _____slowness_____ caused us to be late.

8. I will remember the _____coldness_____ of that winter for a long time.

B **Find the missing letters. Then write the word.**

1. <u>s</u> <u>l</u> o <u>w</u> <u>n</u> e <u>s</u> <u>s</u>   _____slowness_____

2. <u>l</u> o u <u>d</u> <u>n</u> e <u>s</u> <u>s</u>   _____loudness_____

3. c o <u>l</u> d <u>n</u> e <u>s</u> <u>s</u>   _____coldness_____

C **Circle the word that is the same as the top one.**

<u>sickness</u>	<u>darkness</u>	<u>fairness</u>	<u>kindness</u>	<u>blackness</u>
sichness	barkness	fainress	kimdness	blachness
sickmess	dankness	(fairness)	kinbness	blockness
(sickness)	(darkness)	tairness	hindness	blackmess
siekness	darhness	foirness	(kindness)	(blackness)

Name _____

Words with -*ness*

slowness	coldness	fairness	blackness
sickness	darkness	kindness	loudness

A Circle the suffix in each spelling word.

slow(ness)   cold(ness)   fair(ness)   loud(ness)

sick(ness)   dark(ness)   kind(ness)   black(ness)

B Which spelling word might be used in discussing each topic?

fairness   **1.** an umpire of a baseball game

sickness   **2.** a patient in a hospital

loudness   **3.** a band at a concert

kindness   **4.** a generous friend

darkness   **5.** a scary night

slowness   **6.** a turtle race

coldness   **7.** a freezer

C Fill in each blank with a spelling word.

1. The opposite of "warmth" is _____coldness_____.

2. Flu is one kind of _____sickness_____.

3. Warmhearted, helpful, and thoughtful describe the state

of _____kindness_____.

4. The word whose root word is a color is _____blackness_____.

5. Which words are the opposite of "speed" and "quiet"?

_____slowness_____   _____loudness_____

DAY 3

Words with -ness

slowness	coldness	fairness	blackness
sickness	darkness	kindness	loudness

A Fill in the *first* blank with the correct word. Then fill in the *second* blank with the spelling word that contains the word in the *first* blank.

1. The opposite of "high" is "___low___."   ___slowness___

2. The opposite of "white" is "___black___."   ___blackness___

3. The opposite of "out" is "___in___."   ___kindness___

4. Oxygen is in the ___air___.   ___fairness___

5. The opposite of "young" is "___old___."   ___coldness___

B Fill in the boxes with the correct spelling words.

1. | s | i | c | k | n | e | s | s |

2. | c | o | l | d | n | e | s | s |

3. | f | a | i | r | n | e | s | s |

4. | b | l | a | c | k | n | e | s | s |

5. | l | o | u | d | n | e | s | s |

6. | d | a | r | k | n | e | s | s |

7. | s | l | o | w | n | e | s | s |

8. | k | i | n | d | n | e | s | s |

C Write the spelling words in alphabetical order.

1. ___blackness___   2. ___coldness___   3. ___darkness___

4. ___fairness___   5. ___kindness___   6. ___loudness___

7. ___sickness___   8. ___slowness___

Name _____

Words with -ness

slowness	coldness	fairness	blackness
sickness	darkness	kindness	loudness

A Use the correct spelling words to complete the poem.

In the black _____darkness_____ of night, I can barely see

A mysterious ship that beckons to me.

It sails with such _____slowness_____, hardly moving at all,

Riding dark waves that rise and fall.

The sails are lowered; the ship glides away.

Was it real or a dream? I don't think I could say.

B Find each hidden word from the list.

slowness	kindness	sameness
sickness	blackness	quietness
coldness	loudness	lightness
darkness	fairness	wetness

```
n  e  q  u  i  e  t  n  e  s  s  n  e  s  d
b  l  a  c  k  n  e  s  s  a  l  i  c  s  a
l  i  w  f  a  i  r  f  n  m  o  c  o  m  r
o  g  e  s  l  o  w  a  e  e  w  e  l  a  k
u  h  t  w  e  t  n  i  s  n  n  n  d  l  n
d  t  n  d  a  r  k  r  s  e  e  e  n  l  e
n  n  e  k  i  n  d  n  e  s  s  h  e  n  s
e  e  s  l  o  w  n  e  s  s  e  n  s  e  s
s  s  s  a  m  e  n  s  e  n  e  e  s  s  e
s  s  i  c  k  n  e  s  s  b  l  s  a  c  k
```

depart	descend	hopeful	peaceful	fair
decide	decrease	careful	beautiful	fare
deflate	deliver	truthful	thoughtful	it's
deposit	dehydrate	harmful	thankful	its

A Write a spelling word under each picture.

1. _____fair_____   2. _____deliver_____   3. _____deposit_____

B Fill in each blank with a spelling word.

1. The dog licked _____its_____ sore paw.

2. I am _____hopeful_____ that I will pass the test.

3. Your body may _____dehydrate_____ if you don't drink enough fluids.

4. We had to _____descend_____ a very steep stairway at her house.

5. I'm _____thankful_____ my sister is my best friend.

6. How much is the bus _____fare_____ to Washington?

7. I have to _____decide_____ if I'm leaving today or tomorrow.

8. Please be _____careful_____ if you are going to drive in the rain.

9. You should always be _____truthful_____ about how you feel.

10. The train will _____depart_____ at six o'clock.

11. A bad sunburn is _____harmful_____ to a person's skin.

12. My bicycle tire is beginning to _____deflate_____ because I ran over a nail.

Name _____

useless	careless	sickness	slowness	thrown
harmless	hopeless	coldness	fairness	throne
painless	thankless	darkness	kindness	shown
helpless	thoughtless	loudness	blackness	shone

C **Find the missing letters. Then write the word.**

1. __k__ i n __d__ __n__ e __s__ s   kindness

2. p a __i__ __n__ l __e__ __s__ s   painless

3. t __h__ __r__ __o__ __w__ n   thrown

4. s __h__ __o__ __n__ e   shone

5. c o __l__ __d__ n e __s__ __s__   coldness

6. __c__ a r __e__ l __e__ __s__ s   careless

D **Use the correct spelling words to complete the story.**

My parents did not want a puppy. My brother and I tried to talk them into

getting one, but it was _____useless_____ . We had not _____shown_____

them that we could take care of a _____helpless_____ animal.

Then one day we stopped at an animal shelter. The sound of the barking

dogs made it hard to think! Trying to pick one puppy seemed _____hopeless_____

because they were all so cute. But the look on one dog's face and the

_____blackness_____ of her fur helped us to decide once and for all. We said we

would care for her in _____sickness_____ and in health. Then my parents said we

could keep her!

Homonyms

plain	past	forth	stake
plane	passed	fourth	steak

A Fill in each blank with a spelling word.

1. My family has lived here for the _____past_____ five years.

2. She pounded the tent _____stake_____ with a hammer.

3. This is the _____fourth_____ summer I have mowed lawns.

4. He was happy because he had _____passed_____ the spelling test.

5. The coach paced back and _____forth_____ in front of the bench.

6. At 4:00 P.M., the _____plane_____ will depart for Portland.

7. The package arrived in a _____plain_____ brown box.

8. Our Sunday dinner will be _____steak_____ and potatoes.

B Fill in the boxes with the correct spelling words.

1.  s t e a k

2. s t a k e

3. 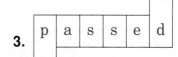 p a s s e d

4. f o r t h

5. p l a i n

6. f o u r t h

7. p l a n e

8. p a s t

C Write the spelling words that have a long *a* sound.

1. _____plain_____   2. _____plane_____

3. _____stake_____   4. _____steak_____

Name _____

Homonyms

plain	past	forth	stake
plane	passed	fourth	steak

A Find the missing letters. Then write the word.

1. p _a_ _s_ s _e_ _d_   _____passed_____

2. _f_ _o_ r _t_ _h_   _____forth_____

3. _p_ l _a_ _n_ e   _____plane_____

B Use the correct spelling words to complete the story.

Each summer, on the _____fourth_____ of June, we have a family reunion.

For the _____past_____ ten years, we've gathered at my grandparents' home.

Most of us drive to the reunion. But my cousins have to come by

_____plane_____. They live hundreds of miles away.

It's nearly time for our next reunion. I can hardly believe a year has

_____passed_____ since the last one. I can't wait to see everyone!

C Write the correct spelling word beside each clue.

_____stake_____	**1.** a piece of wood or metal
_____plane_____	**2.** a vehicle for air travel
_____plain_____	**3.** ordinary, clear, or simple
_____passed_____	**4.** moved on or by (verb)
_____steak_____	**5.** meat
_____fourth_____	**6.** the one after third
_____forth_____	**7.** forward
_____past_____	**8.** gone by (adjective)

Lesson 16 Homonyms

plain	past	forth	stake
plane	passed	fourth	steak

A Write the spelling words in alphabetical order.

1. _____forth_____ 2. _____fourth_____ 3. _____passed_____

4. _____past_____ 5. _____plain_____ 6. _____plane_____

7. _____stake_____ 8. _____steak_____

B Fill in each blank with a spelling word.

1. We biked _____past_____ the beautiful garden.

2. How do you like your _____steak_____ cooked?

3. We _____passed_____ a slow-moving car on the highway.

4. My cousin is in the _____fourth_____ grade.

C Circle the word that is the same as the top one.

plain	plane	passed	fourth	forth	stake
plian	palne	pased	fourtk	fonth	(stake)
plaim	(plane)	passeb	fonrth	(forth)	slake
glain	plame	passcd	founth	farth	stoke
(plain)	plone	(passed)	(fourth)	forfh	stahe

D Write a spelling word under each picture.

1. _____plane_____ 2. _____stake_____ 3. _____steak_____

Name _____

Homonyms

plain	past	forth	stake
plane	passed	fourth	steak

A Use each spelling word in a sentence.

plain _____

past _____

passed _____

forth _____

stake _____

fourth _____

B Find each hidden word from the list.

plain	main	grain	train	brain
plane	crane	sane	lane	vane
past	cast	fast	mast	last
stake	brake	flake	rake	make
steak	break	forth	fourth	passed

```
p  l  a  i  n  a  b  r  a  k  e  f  a  s  t
p  a  s  s  e  d  m  a  i  n  p  o  b  a  r
o  n  c  t  r  a  a  k  e  g  l  u  r  i  a
f  e  a  a  s  a  n  e  a  r  a  r  e  p  i
l  a  s  k  m  a  k  e  p  a  s  t  a  m  n
a  s  t  e  a  k  a  b  l  i  e  h  k  s  l
k  a  s  t  s  e  c  r  a  n  e  l  e  d  e
e  f  o  r  t  h  r  a  n  e  m  a  c  e  s
g  r  a  i  t  e  n  i  e  n  o  s  n  d  t
s  t  e  a  h  v  a  n  e  e  a  t  a  i  e
```

DAY 1

Words with *-ly*

friendly	correctly	quickly	safely
honestly	partly	quietly	bravely

A **Fill in each blank with a spelling word.**

1. To make sure you ride _____safely_____, keep your seat belt on.

2. Our _____friendly_____ neighbors invited us to dinner.

3. She tiptoed _____quietly_____ out of the room.

4. The man _____bravely_____ risked his life to save the others.

5. The forecaster said the weather would be _____partly_____ cloudy.

6. He answered the question _____correctly_____ and passed the test.

7. We _____honestly_____ didn't know what to do next.

8. Let's take the short cut, to get there _____quickly_____.

B **Fill in the boxes with the correct spelling words.**

1. h o n e s t l y

2. c o r r e c t l y

3. q u i c k l y

4. f r i e n d l y

5. s a f e l y

6. p a r t l y

7. b r a v e l y

8. q u i e t l y

C **Write the spelling words that have three syllables.**

_____correctly_____   _____honestly_____   _____quietly_____

Name _____

Words with -*ly*

friendly	correctly	quickly	safely
honestly	partly	quietly	bravely

A Fill in each blank with a spelling word.

1. Write the word that begins with a silent letter. ___honestly___

2. Write the words that have a short *e* sound.

   ___friendly___   ___quietly___

   ___correctly___   ___honestly___

3. Write the two shortest words.

   ___safely___   ___partly___

B Find the missing letters. Then write the word.

1. q _u_ _i_ c _k_ _l_ _y_   ___quickly___

2. _p_ _a_ r _t_ _l_ y   ___partly___

3. _f_ _r_ _i_ e _n_ _d_ l _y_   ___friendly___

4. _c_ _o_ _r_ r _e_ _c_ t _l_ y   ___correctly___

C Circle the suffix in each spelling word.

friend(ly)   hones(tly)   correc(tly)   par(tly)

quick(ly)   quie(tly)   saf(ely)   brave(ly)

D Write the spelling words in alphabetical order.

1. ___bravely___   2. ___correctly___   3. ___friendly___

4. ___honestly___   5. ___partly___   6. ___quickly___

7. ___quietly___   8. ___safely___

Words with *-ly*

friendly	correctly	quickly	safely
honestly	partly	quietly	bravely

A Write the spelling word that matches its antonym (opposite).

1. slowly   _____quickly_____

2. dangerously   _____safely_____

3. completely   _____partly_____

4. dishonestly   _____honestly_____

5. cowardly   _____bravely_____

6. unfriendly   _____friendly_____

B Put an *X* on the word that is <u>not</u> the same.

1. friendly	fre~~i~~ndly	friendly	friendly	friendly
2. quietly	quietly	qu~~ie~~tly	quietly	quietly
3. partly	pa~~r~~ty	partly	partly	partly
4. safely	safely	safely	safely	saf~~e~~ty

C Use each spelling word in a sentence.

correctly _____

safely _____

honestly _____

quietly _____

quickly _____

bravely _____

Name _____

75

Words with -ly

| friendly | correctly | quickly | safely |
| honestly | partly | quietly | bravely |

A Circle the word that is the same as the top one.

friendly	honestly	quietly	correctly	bravely
freindly	homestly	guietly	cornectly	(bravely)
friemdly	honsetly	quielty	(correctly)	dravely
fniendly	(honestly)	(quietly)	correclty	bnavely
(friendly)	lonestly	qniety	carrectly	braevly

B Use the correct spelling words to complete the story.

My neighbor's dog had seven puppies. I chose one of them to keep.

The choice wasn't easy, though. Every one of the pups was lovable and

_____friendly_____.

When the puppies saw me coming, they _____quickly_____ scrambled

toward me. They cried and whined for attention.

I _____honestly_____ don't know how I was able to choose just one of

the puppies.

C Complete each sentence.

1. It was partly _____.

2. She quickly _____.

3. We went safely _____.

4. Honestly, I _____.

Words with -*ment*

statement	equipment	enjoyment	encouragement
argument	payment	retirement	advertisement

A Fill in each blank with a spelling word. (The suffix *ment* indicates action or result.)

1. We need _____ equipment _____ for our new gym.

2. Did you see the _____ advertisement _____ for ripe peaches?

3. Her _____ enjoyment _____ of dancing lasted many years.

4. After fifty years of work, she was ready for _____ retirement _____.

5. The president issued a _____ statement _____ on the crisis.

6. The cheering of the crowd gave the runner great
   _____ encouragement _____.

7. My mother settled the _____ argument _____ between my sister and myself.

8. Our rent _____ payment _____ is due the first day of each month.

B Find the missing letters. Then write the word.

1. e _n_ _j_ _o_ y _m_ e _n_ t   _____ enjoyment _____

2. _a_ r _g_ u _m_ e _n_ _t_   _____ argument _____

3. _r_ _e_ t _i_ _r_ e _m_ e _n_ _t_   _____ retirement _____

C Fill in each blank with a spelling word.

1. Write the words with two syllables.

   _____ payment _____   _____ statement _____

2. Write the words with four syllables.

   _____ advertisement _____   _____ encouragement _____

Name _____

Lesson 18

DAY 2

Words with -*ment*

statement	equipment	enjoyment	encouragement
argument	payment	retirement	advertisement

A Write the spelling words in alphabetical order.

1. advertisement
2. argument
3. encouragement
4. enjoyment
5. equipment
6. payment
7. retirement
8. statement

B Which spelling word might be used in discussing each topic?

encouragement	**1.**	cheering at a sports event
payment, statement	**2.**	rent or telephone bill
equipment	**3.**	furnishing a gym
argument	**4.**	debate
advertisement	**5.**	TV commercial

C Fill in the boxes with the correct spelling words.

1. p a y m e n t

2. a d v e r t i s e m e n t

3. a r g u m e n t

4. e n c o u r a g e m e n t

5. e n j o y m e n t

6. e q u i p m e n t

7. r e t i r e m e n t

8. s t a t e m e n t

DAY
3

Words with -*ment*

| statement | equipment | enjoyment | encouragement |
| argument | payment | retirement | advertisement |

A Find each hidden word from the list.

statement	enjoyment	environment
argument	advertisement	measurement
equipment	encouragement	employment
payment	retirement	judgment

```
j  u  a  d  v  e  r  t  i  s  e  m  e  n  t
e  q  u  i  p  m  e  n  t  o  t  o  n  p  a
n  e  h  s  t  a  t  e  m  e  n  t  j  a  s
v  i  l  l  e  n  i  o  r  t  h  y  o  y  c
i  m  e  a  s  u  r  e  m  e  n  t  y  m  a
r  a  r  g  u  m  e  n  t  r  o  y  m  e  l
o  i  n  a  u  e  m  p  l  o  y  m  e  n  t
n  j  u  d  g  m  e  n  t  n  i  t  n  t  e
m  d  s  t  a  t  n  e  s  o  f  a  t  m  e
e  r  i  c  a  w  t  o  r  l  d  g  a  l  a
n  x  y  u  n  i  v  e  r  s  e  w  h  a  t
t  e  n  c  o  u  r  a  g  e  m  e  n  t  e
```

B Use each spelling word in a sentence.

statement _____

advertisement _____

encouragement _____

equipment _____

argument _____

Name _____

Words with -*ment*

statement	equipment	enjoyment	encouragement
argument	payment	retirement	advertisement

A Circle the root word in each spelling word.

(advertise)ment   (retire)ment   (equip)ment

(encourage)ment   (enjoy)ment   (pay)ment

B Fill in each blank with the correct word.

1. The suffix for all the spelling words is _____ment_____.

2. All the spelling words are _____nouns_____.
   (nouns, verbs, adverbs)

3. Write the spelling words that begin with a consonant.

   _____statement_____   _____payment_____   _____retirement_____

C Use the correct spelling words to complete the story.

If you retire at the age of sixty or so, what kinds of things will you do?

It's said that many people get the most _____enjoyment_____ out of life

in their _____retirement_____ years. They take up hobbies. They travel

from place to place. Some people go back to school.

There's an _____advertisement_____ on TV about volunteer work for

retirees. You work in a place, such as a hospital, for a few hours a week.

You give your time without receiving any _____payment_____. If you

plan for retirement, it can be the best time of your life.

Lesson 19

Homonyms

| doe | peer | air | bass |
| dough | pier | heir | base |

A Fill in each blank with a spelling word.

1. The fawn followed the _____doe_____ into the meadow.

2. He hit the ball and ran to first _____base_____.

3. You can _____peer_____ into this telescope.

4. A person who by law comes to own something from another person is called an _____heir_____.

5. The boat was tied to the _____pier_____.

6. He plays _____bass_____ guitar in a rock band.

7. The _____air_____ at the beach smells salty.

8. He made whole wheat _____dough_____ for the bread.

B Fill in the boxes with the correct spelling words.

1. b a s s

2. p e e r

3. b a s e

4. d o u g h

5. p i e r

6. a i r

7. d o e

8. h e i r

C Which spelling word has more than one pronunciation?

_____bass_____

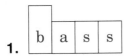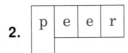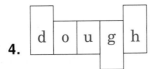

Name _____

81

Homonyms

doe	peer	air	bass
dough	pier	heir	base

A Find the missing letters. Then write the word.

1. h e i r _____ heir _____

2. d o u g h _____ dough _____

B Write the correct spelling word beside each clue.

_____ peer _____	**1.** to look at
_____ heir _____	**2.** a person who inherits something
_____ base _____	**3.** bottom
_____ bass _____	**4.** a singer with a deep voice
_____ dough _____	**5.** a mixture of flour and water
_____ doe _____	**6.** a female deer
_____ pier _____	**7.** a dock
_____ air _____	**8.** the gases we breathe

C Write the spelling words in alphabetical order.

1. _____ air _____   2. _____ base _____   3. _____ bass _____   4. _____ doe _____

5. _____ dough _____   6. _____ heir _____   7. _____ peer _____   8. _____ pier _____

D Write a spelling word under each picture.

1. _____ pier _____   2. _____ base _____   3. _____ doe _____

Lesson 19 **Homonyms**

doe	peer	air	bass
dough	pier	heir	base

A Use the correct spelling words to complete the story.

A man prepared for a day of sailing in his new boat. He stood on the

dock awhile to _____peer_____ at the beautiful blue sky. The shapes of the

clouds told him about the weather. The _____air_____ around him had a

sharp bite to it, but he was dressed warmly.

He walked to the end of the _____pier_____ toward his sailboat.

He thought it would be a fine day for a sail.

B Below are guide words. Write the spelling word that would come between each pair in the dictionary.

_____peer_____ **1.** pace—phone

_____doe_____ **2.** doctor—done

_____bass_____ **3.** basket—bath

_____heir_____ **4.** heat—hire

C Put an *X* on the word that is <u>not</u> the same.

1. pier	pier	~~peir~~	pier	pier
2. dough	dough	dough	~~dough~~	dough
3. heir	heir	heir	heir	~~hier~~
4. base	base	base	~~basc~~	base
5. air	~~ain~~	air	air	air

Name _____

Homonyms

doe	peer	air	bass
dough	pier	heir	base

A Circle the word that is the same as the top one.

dough	pier	doe	heir	bass	base
doguh	peir	boe	hier	bas	bose
bough	gier	dae	hein	boss	baes
(dough)	peer	(doe)	leir	(bass)	dase
daugh	(pier)	doc	(heir)	dass	(base)

B Write a paragraph using four of the spelling words.

_____

_____

_____

_____

_____

_____

C Fill in each blank with a spelling word.

1. The three-letter words are _____doe_____ and _____air_____.

2. _____Bass_____ ends with a double consonant.

3. Which words each contain the vowels *e* and *i*?

   _____pier_____   _____heir_____

4. _____Dough_____ ends with a silent *h*.

5. The word with a double vowel is _____peer_____.

Words with *-ible*

possible	edible	terrible	visible
horrible	audible	incredible	sensible

A Fill in each blank with a spelling word. (The suffix *ible* means "capable of" or "worthy of.")

1. It's _____sensible_____ to take a compass when you go for a hike.

2. Her voice was so low, it was barely _____audible_____.

3. Is it _____possible_____ that we may arrive early?

4. The acrobat performed many _____incredible_____ feats.

5. That horror movie wasn't so _____horrible_____.

6. Last night we had a _____terrible_____ thunderstorm.

7. The mountain peak is barely _____visible_____ today.

8. Do you think that the leftover food is _____edible_____?

B Find the missing letters. Then write the word.

1. t _e_ r r _i_ b _l_ e   _____terrible_____

2. _h_ o r r _i_ _b_ l e   _____horrible_____

3. _v_ _i_ s _i_ b l e   _____visible_____

4. _s_ e n s _i_ b l e   _____sensible_____

C Circle the word that is the same as the top one.

edible	audible	possible	sensible	incredible
ebidle	aubidle	posslbile	sersible	increbible
edidle	(audible)	passible	(sensible)	incredibel
(edible)	audibel	(possible)	seusible	incerdible
edibel	andible	gossible	sensidle	(incredible)

Name _____

DAY 2

Words with *-ible*

| possible | edible | terrible | visible |
| horrible | audible | incredible | sensible |

A Write the spelling words in alphabetical order.

1. _____audible_____   2. _____edible_____

3. _____horrible_____   4. _____incredible_____

5. _____possible_____   6. _____sensible_____

7. _____terrible_____   8. _____visible_____

B Circle the suffix in each spelling word.

poss(ible)   terr(ible)   vis(ible)   aud(ible)

horr(ible)   incred(ible)   sens(ible)   ed(ible)

C Complete each sentence with a spelling word.

1. If something can be seen, it is _____visible_____.

2. If something can be heard, it is _____audible_____.

3. If something can be eaten, it is _____edible_____.

4. If something is unbelievable, it is _____incredible_____.

5. If something is capable of happening, it is _____possible_____.

6. If something makes good sense, it is _____sensible_____.

D Fill in each blank with a spelling word.

1. Write the word with four syllables. _____incredible_____

2. Write the words that begin with vowels.

_____audible_____   _____incredible_____   _____edible_____

DAY
3

Words with *-ible*

| possible | edible | terrible | visible |
| horrible | audible | incredible | sensible |

A Fill in the boxes with the correct spelling words.

1. t e r r i b l e

2. i n c r e d i b l e

3. s e n s i b l e

4. v i s i b l e

5. h o r r i b l e

6. a u d i b l e

7. p o s s i b l e

8. e d i b l e

B Write the spelling word that matches its antonym (opposite).

1. believable   incredible

2. wonderful   horrible or terrible

3. inedible   edible

4. not reasonable   sensible

5. unseen   visible

C Choose a spelling word that can describe each noun.

1. horrible, terrible fire   2. edible mushrooms

3. possible rain   4. sensible agreement

5. audible whistle   6. incredible rainbow

Name _____

Words with -ible

| possible | edible | terrible | visible |
| horrible | audible | incredible | sensible |

A Use each spelling word in a sentence.

possible _____

sensible _____

edible _____

terrible _____

visible _____

incredible _____

audible _____

horrible _____

B Use the correct spelling words to complete the story.

Hundreds of years ago, people had to travel on land for thousands of

miles to get from Europe to India. Most people thought it was not

_____possible_____ to get there faster by sea. But a man named

Christopher Columbus thought he could find a route to India by sea. He

asked the king and queen of Spain for money for his journey.

After more than a month at sea, his crew was running out of drinking

water and _____edible_____ food. Then, on October 12, 1492, what we

know as the Bahama Islands became _____visible_____. He had not

found India, but had discovered a world new to him.

Columbus made four trips in all to try to find a route to India. Although

he never succeeded, Christopher Columbus is an important part of history.

partly	friendly	statement	payment	air
safely	honestly	encouragement	steak	heir
bravely	correctly	advertisement	base	plane
quietly	quickly	retirement	pier	bass

A **Write a spelling word under each picture.**

1. _____steak_____   2. _____plane_____   3. _____pier_____

B **Fill in each blank with a spelling word.**

1. With the ___encouragement___ of friends, he was successful.

2. We walked ___quietly___ so that we would not scare the deer.

3. He made it home ___safely___ during the snowstorm.

4. The ___base___ of the sculpture was made of stone.

5. She made a brave ___statement___ to the class.

6. I am ___partly___ responsible for what happened.

7. Who is the ___heir___ to England's throne?

8. My cat is very sweet and ___friendly___ .

9. She answered each question ___correctly___ and passed the test.

10. His car ___payment___ is due every month.

11. The movie is about to start, so we should leave ___quickly___ .

12. My grandparents are enjoying their ___retirement___ .

Name _____

plain	passed	stake	edible	sensible
enjoyment	past	doe	audible	possible
argument	forth	dough	visible	horrible
equipment	fourth	peer	terrible	incredible

C **Find the missing letters. Then write the word.**

1. d o __u__ __g__ __h__   dough

2. s __t__ __a__ k __e__   stake

3. __p__ __a__ s __t__   past

4. __p__ l __a__ __i__ __n__   plain

5. p __e__ __e__ r   peer

6. __p__ a s __s__ __e__ __d__   passed

7. i __n__ c __r__ e __d__ ib __l__ e   incredible

D **Use the correct spelling words to complete the story.**

Some people like to hear scary stories or watch horror movies. They like to be frightened by __horrible, terrible__ movie scenes filled with terror. Sometimes people are terrified by something that is __visible__ on the screen like a ghost. Sometimes just a sound that is barely __audible__ is enough to scare them.

I don't understand how anyone can watch scary movies. If I see a scary movie, I cover my eyes so that I can't see what is happening. I think it is much more __sensible__ to watch an adventure movie or one that is romantic. Then it is __possible__ to have sweet dreams instead of nightmares!

Words with -*able*

likable	usable	movable	lovable
believable	returnable	valuable	breakable

A Fill in each blank with a spelling word.

1. The job applicant seemed _____likable_____ and experienced.

2. Save that bottle because it's _____returnable_____ at the store.

3. The log was so heavy, it was barely _____movable_____.

4. Is that a nonbreakable or _____breakable_____ jar?

5. His story sounded _____believable_____, but it wasn't true.

6. If you recycle paper, it's _____usable_____ more than once.

7. What a _____lovable_____ puppy!

8. Gold is more _____valuable_____ than silver.

B Fill in the boxes with the correct spelling words.

1.  m o v a b l e

2. 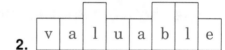 v a l u a b l e

3.  b r e a k a b l e

4. 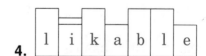 l i k a b l e

5. 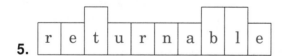 r e t u r n a b l e

6.  l o v a b l e

7. 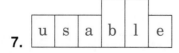 u s a b l e

8. b e l i e v a b l e

C Write the spelling words that have four syllables.

_____returnable_____   _____valuable_____   _____believable_____

Name_____

DAY 2

Words with -*able*

likable	usable	movable	lovable
believable	returnable	valuable	breakable

A Circle the suffix in each spelling word.

lik(able) believ(able) us(able) return(able)

mov(able) valu(able) lov(able) break(able)

B Write the root word of each spelling word. (In each of the root words, the silent *e* was dropped before the suffix *able* was added. Example: size + able = sizable.)

1. likable _____like_____   **2.** valuable _____value_____

3. movable _____move_____   **4.** usable _____use_____

5. believable ____believe____   **6.** lovable _____love_____

C Circle the word that is the same as the top one.

likable	usable	movable	lovable	valuable
likabel	usabel	(movable)	lavoble	(valuable)
likeble	(usable)	movadle	lovabel	valuadle
(likable)	usoble	mowable	(lovable)	valuabel

D Answer each question with a spelling word.

1. Which word has five vowels? _____believable_____

2. Which word begins with a vowel? _____usable_____

3. Which word has a long *i* sound? _____likable_____

4. Which word has a long *a* sound? _____breakable_____

Words with -able

| likable | usable | movable | lovable |
| believable | returnable | valuable | breakable |

A Find the missing letters. Then write the word.

1. r e t u r n a b l e   returnable

2. u s a b l e   usable

3. l i k a b l e   likable

4. m o v a b l e   movable

B Put an *X* on the word that is <u>not</u> the same.

1. likable	likable	likable	li~~h~~able	likable
2. believable	believable	belie~~v~~able	believable	believable
3. usable	usable	usable	usa~~d~~le	usable
4. returnable	returnable	returnable	returnable	retur~~n~~oble
5. movable	movable	mo~~v~~able	movable	movable
6. valuable	valuable	valuable	vala~~u~~ble	valuable
7. lovable	lovable	lovable	lovable	lova~~d~~le
8. breakable	bra~~e~~kable	breakable	breakable	breakable

C Choose a spelling word that can describe each noun.

1. usable, valuable tools

2. breakable glass

3. movable furniture

4. believable story

5. valuable diamond

6. lovable, likable kitten

Name _____

DAY 4

Words with -able

likable	usable	movable	lovable
believable	returnable	valuable	breakable

A **Use the correct spelling words to complete the story.**

I once had a teacher who asked our class to list the best things about ourselves. "Make your list _____believable_____," she said. "Make your list sound just the way you are."

Some of us didn't know what to write. She used the lesson to show us how to look for our most _____likable_____ qualities. It turned out to be a very _____valuable_____ lesson.

B **Complete each sentence with a spelling word.**

1. If something can be broken, it's _____breakable_____.

2. If something can be moved from one spot to another, it's _____movable_____.

3. If something is enjoyable, it's _____likable_____.

4. If a story is worthy of belief, it's _____believable_____.

5. If something can be taken back, it's _____returnable_____.

6. If something has much worth, it's _____valuable_____.

C **Write the spelling words in alphabetical order.**

1. _____believable_____

2. _____breakable_____

3. _____likable_____

4. _____lovable_____

5. _____movable_____

6. _____returnable_____

7. _____usable_____

8. _____valuable_____

Homonyms

patience	threw	who's	your
patients	through	whose	you're

A Fill in each blank with a spelling word.

1. _____Who's_____ going to the game with us?

2. She _____threw_____ the ball over the fence.

3. _____You're_____ going to do well today!

4. The two _____patients_____ shared a hospital room.

5. We hiked _____through_____ the forest to the waterfall.

6. It takes _____patience_____ to do a jigsaw puzzle.

7. Do you know _____whose_____ car that is?

8. _____Your_____ mother is very thoughtful.

B Find the missing letters. Then write the word.

1. t _h_ _r_ _e_ _w_   _____threw_____

2. _y_ _o_ _u_ r   _____your_____

3. _w_ h _o_ ' _s_   _____who's_____

4. _p_ _a_ t _i_ _e_ _n_ t _s_   _____patients_____

C Circle the word that is the same as the top one.

patience	patients	through	whose	you're
pateince	patienls	throuqh	(whose)	yon're
patiemce	(patients)	thruogh	wkose	you'er
(patience)	gatients	thnough	whase	(you're)
potience	pateints	(through)	whoes	your'e

Name _____

Homonyms

patience	threw	who's	your
patients	through	whose	you're

A Write the spelling words in alphabetical order.

1. _patience_   2. _patients_   3. _threw_

4. _through_   5. _who's_   6. _whose_

7. _your_   8. _you're_

B Fill in each blank with the correct word.

1. "Threw" and _through_ are homonyms.

2. "Whose" and _who's_ are homonyms.

3. "Your" and "you're" are _homonyms_.

4. "Patience" and _patients_ are _homonyms_.

C Fill in the blanks with "who's" or "whose." ("Who's" is a contraction of "who is" or "who has." "Whose" is used to show possession or ownership.)

1. _Who's_ coming to our house?

2. _Whose_ dog is the black one?

3. I know _who's_ going to the dance.

4. Do you know anyone _who's_ been to China?

5. _Whose_ pencil is this one?

6. _Who's_ allowed to go to the movies?

7. I'm not sure _whose_ car that is.

8. _Who's_ coming over for dinner?

Homonyms

patience	threw	who's	your
patients	through	whose	you're

A Fill in the boxes with the correct spelling words.

1. t h r e w

2. y o u ' r e

3. p a t i e n t s

4. w h o ' s

5. p a t i e n c e

6. w h o s e

7. y o u r

8. t h r o u g h

B Fill in the blanks with "you're" or "your." ("You're" is a contraction of "you are." "Your" is used to show ownership or possession.)

1. _____Your_____ horse is well trained.

2. I see _____you're_____ wearing the hat I gave you.

3. _____You're_____ supposed to watch _____your_____ sister today.

4. Is the party at _____your_____ house?

5. _____You're_____ doing a great job of painting the room!

6. _____You're_____ the best swimmer on our team.

7. It's time for _____your_____ favorite TV show.

8. Have you decided what _____you're_____ going to do this summer?

Name _____

Homonyms

patience	threw	who's	your
patients	through	whose	you're

A Complete each phrase with a spelling word.

1. a doctor who visits _____patients_____ in their homes

2. _____threw_____ a baseball to the batter

3. drove _____through_____ the tunnel

4. the _____patience_____ of taking one step at a time

5. too dark to see where _____you're_____ going

6. find _____your_____ way back home

7. an idea _____whose_____ time has come

8. a person _____who's_____ willing to take a stand

B Use the correct spelling words to complete the story.

You're a great baseball player. _____Your_____ pitching arm is very strong; you once _____threw_____ three no-hitters in a row. You have a lot of _____patience_____ with new players, teaching them how to improve their ball game. _____Who's_____ better at bat than you? Not many can hit as well as you. For a player _____whose_____ career in baseball is just beginning, _____you're_____ terrific!

C Fill in each blank with the correct word.

1. _____You're_____ is a contraction of "you are."

2. "Who's" is a _____contraction_____ of "who is" or "who has."

3. The words _____whose_____ and _____your_____ show ownership.

DAY 1

Words with *-tion*

| caution | education | affection | transportation |
| direction | protection | operation | construction |

A **Fill in each blank with a spelling word. (The suffix *tion* means "action involved with.")**

1. The best _____transportation_____ here is the subway.

2. The _____operation_____ to repair his shoulder was successful.

3. A well-rounded _____education_____ connects you to the world.

4. Do you know from what _____direction_____ the wind is blowing?

5. _____Construction_____ has begun on the new house.

6. I show a lot of _____affection_____ to my cat.

7. Drivers should use _____caution_____ on icy roads.

8. I wear a hat outdoors for _____protection_____ from the sun.

B **Write the spelling words in alphabetical order.**

1. _____affection_____   2. _____caution_____

3. _____construction_____   4. _____direction_____

5. _____education_____   6. _____operation_____

7. _____protection_____   8. _____transportation_____

C **Fill in each blank with a spelling word.**

1. Write the words that have five vowels.

_____education_____   _____transportation_____   _____operation_____

2. Write the words that have four syllables.

_____education_____   _____transportation_____   _____operation_____

Name _____

Words with -tion

| caution | education | affection | transportation |
| direction | protection | operation | construction |

A Use the correct spelling words to complete the story.

Our state government is responsible for doing many things. The

_____transportation_____ of people from place to place is a big concern of

the state. The state plans the _____construction_____ of new roads. It

has to help build schools for the _____education_____ of its citizens.

And its people need _____protection_____ from crime.

Running a state government is very complex. People with different

talents must communicate and work together for its smooth

_____operation_____.

B Find the missing letters. Then write the word.

1. _d_ _i_ r _e_ _c_ _t_ i _o_ _n_   _____direction_____

2. _a_ f _f_ _e_ _c_ t _i_ _o_ _n_   _____affection_____

3. _c_ _a_ u _t_ _i_ _o_ n   _____caution_____

C Which spelling word might be used in discussing each topic?

_____construction_____   **1.** building a tower

_____operation_____   **2.** surgery

_____transportation_____   **3.** planes, trains, and cars

_____protection_____   **4.** umbrellas and raincoats

_____education_____   **5.** schools and universities

Lesson 23

Words with *-tion*

DAY 3

| caution | education | affection | transportation |
| direction | protection | operation | construction |

A Use each spelling word in a sentence.

caution _____

protection _____

affection _____

direction _____

B Write the spelling word that matches its antonym (opposite).

1. destruction _____construction_____

2. dislike _____affection_____

3. ignorance _____education_____

4. recklessness _____caution_____

C Write a spelling word under each picture.

 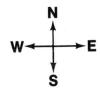

1. _____construction_____ **2.** _____direction_____ **3.** _____affection_____

D Fill in each blank with the correct word.

1. "Transport" is the root word of _____transportation_____.

2. _____Protect_____ is the root word of "protection."

3. "Operate" is the root word of _____operation_____.

4. _____Educate_____ is the root word of "education."

Name _____

DAY 4

Words with *-tion*

caution	education	affection	transportation
direction	protection	operation	construction

A Use spelling words to complete the puzzle.

Across

2. taking care of something

4. being careful

5. bicycles, cars, ships, and trains

8. the act of directing

Down

1. the act of building

3. instruction

6. a fond or tender feeling

7. a process, or the act of working

		1 c			2 p	r	o	3 e	c	t	i	o	n

Crossword grid:
- 1 Down (starting col): c, o, n, s
- 2 Across: p r o t e c t i o n
- 3 Down: e, d, (4)c, c
- 4 Across: c a u t i o n
- 5 Across: t r a n s p o r t a t i o n
- 5 Down: t, r, u, c, t, i, o, n
- 6 Down: a, f, f, e, c, t, i, o, n
- 7 Down: o, p, e, r, a, t, i, o, n
- 8 Across: d i r e c t i o n

Lesson 24

Words with -*sion*

| invasion | decision | vision | erosion |
| confusion | television | explosion | collision |

A **Fill in each blank with a spelling word.**

1. An _____invasion_____ of termites weakened the wood.

2. The lack of ground cover caused the soil's _____erosion_____.

3. She made the _____decision_____ to study abroad.

4. The earthquake caused the _____explosion_____ of the gas tanks.

5. When the traffic lights broke, there was _____confusion_____ among the drivers.

6. The _____collision_____ of the waiters caused their trays to spill.

7. I need glasses to correct my _____vision_____.

8. The play was shown on _____television_____ last night.

B **Find the missing letters. Then write the word.**

1. e r o s i o n   _____erosion_____

2. d e c i s i o n   _____decision_____

3. c o n f u s i o n   _____confusion_____

4. i n v a s i o n   _____invasion_____

C **Write a spelling word under each picture.**

1. _____television_____   2. _____confusion_____   3. _____collision_____

Name _____

Lesson 24

Words with -*sion*

invasion	decision	vision	erosion
confusion	television	explosion	collision

A Fill in the boxes with the correct spelling words.

1.  e r o s i o n

2. 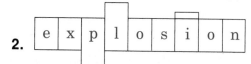 e x p l o s i o n

3. 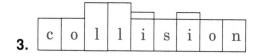 c o l l i s i o n

4.  i n v a s i o n

5. c o n f u s i o n

6. 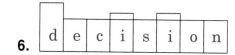 d e c i s i o n

B Write the correct spelling word beside each clue.

collision	**1.** crash
erosion	**2.** wearing away
vision	**3.** sight
invasion	**4.** entrance by force
decision	**5.** the process of deciding
confusion	**6.** disorder
television	**7.** a form of entertainment
explosion	**8.** a violent release of energy

C Answer each question with a spelling word.

1. Which spelling word appears in another spelling word?

   vision

2. Which word does it appear in?   television

Words with -*sion*

invasion	decision	vision	erosion
confusion	television	explosion	collision

A **Find each hidden word from the list.**

invasion	vision	division
confusion	explosion	transfusion
decision	erosion	conclusion
television	collision	provision

```
i  t  r  a  n  s  f  u  s  i  o  n  x  p  x
n  e  x  p  l  o  s  i  o  n  f  x  d  r  i
v  l  x  d  t  e  c  o  n  f  u  s  i  o  n
d  e  c  i  s  i  o  n  t  e  s  l  v  v  v
a  v  a  v  a  s  l  c  v  h  i  e  i  i  a
v  i  s  i  o  n  l  l  s  i  o  n  s  s  s
i  s  i  s  c  i  i  u  s  i  n  o  o  i  i
s  i  o  i  d  e  s  s  i  n  c  l  u  o  o
i  o  n  o  n  s  i  i  d  i  v  i  s  n  n
o  n  e  n  o  c  o  n  c  l  u  s  i  o  n
e  r  o  s  i  o  n  n  p  r  o  v  i  s  i
```

B **Fill in each blank with a spelling word.**

1. The root word of this spelling word is "decide." _____decision_____

2. The root word of this spelling word is "erode." _____erosion_____

3. The root word of this spelling word is "confuse." _____confusion_____

4. The root word of this spelling word is "collide." _____collision_____

5. Write the word that has four syllables. _____television_____

6. Write the word that has two syllables. _____vision_____

Name _____

Words with -*sion*

invasion	decision	vision	erosion
confusion	television	explosion	collision

A Write the spelling words in alphabetical order.

1. _collision_
2. _confusion_
3. _decision_

4. _erosion_
5. _explosion_
6. _invasion_

7. _television_
8. _vision_

B Which spelling word might be used in discussing each topic?

collision 1. a wreck

vision 2. eyeglasses

explosion 3. dynamite

television 4. commercials

invasion 5. war

erosion 6. loss of topsoil

decision 7. which candidate to vote for

C Use the correct spelling words to complete the story.

With the invention of _television_ , the events of the world are

there for us to see. We can share the wonders of life within and beyond our

planet without leaving our homes. We've seen the _explosion_ of

an atom bomb on TV. We watched astronauts play golf on the moon. We

saw the Berlin Wall come down. We've seen hurricanes and floods and their

aftermath. For better or worse, TV has changed our _vision_

of the world.

Words with *-sion*

expansion	mission	extension	possession
permission	tension	admission	comprehension

A Fill in each blank with a spelling word.

1. The math problem was beyond his ___comprehension___.

2. We need an ___extension___ cord for this lamp.

3. An ___admission___ ticket to the concert costs a lot of money.

4. The rancher gave us ___permission___ to swim in her pond.

5. He had twenty-three marbles in his ___possession___.

6. They built an ___expansion___ bridge across the river.

7. The ___mission___ of the group was to create peace.

8. His headache was a result of ___tension___.

B Find the missing letters. Then write the word.

1. <u>t</u> e <u>n</u> <u>s</u> <u>i</u> o <u>n</u>   ___tension___

2. <u>m</u> <u>i</u> s s <u>i</u> <u>o</u> <u>n</u>   ___mission___

3. e <u>x</u> <u>p</u> a <u>n</u> <u>s</u> <u>i</u> <u>o</u> <u>n</u>   ___expansion___

C Put an *X* on the word that is not the same.

1. permission	permission	permission	per~~m~~ision
2. extension	exte~~m~~sion	extension	extension
3. possession	possession	posse~~ss~~oion	possession
4. comprehension	comprehension	comprehension	compre~~h~~ension
5. expansion	expansion	expansion	expa~~n~~sion
6. admission	admission	admission	abm~~i~~ssion

Name _____

Words with *-sion*

| expansion | mission | extension | possession |
| permission | tension | admission | comprehension |

A Fill in the boxes with the correct spelling words.

1. 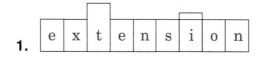 e x t e n s i o n

2. 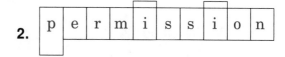 p e r m i s s i o n

3. 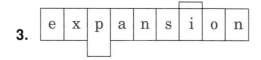 e x p a n s i o n

4.  p o s s e s s i o n

5. a d m i s s i o n

6. 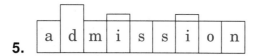 m i s s i o n

B Below are guide words. Write the spelling word that would come between each pair in the dictionary.

_____extension_____ **1.** expenditure—extract

_____expansion_____ **2.** exit—expend

_____possession_____ **3.** permit—post

_____comprehension_____ **4.** advertise—decision

_____tension_____ **5.** possible—terrible

C Write the correct spelling word beside each clue.

_____possession_____ **1.** ownership

_____expansion_____ **2.** growth

_____admission_____ **3.** entrance

_____comprehension_____ **4.** understanding

DAY 3

Words with *-sion*

expansion	mission	extension	possession
permission	tension	admission	comprehension

A Fill in each blank with a spelling word.

_____tension_____ **1.** Add *ex* to this word, and you have another spelling word.

_____mission_____ **2.** Add *ad* to this word, and you have another spelling word.

_____admission_____ **3.** You might see this word on a ticket to a ball game.

_____extension_____ **4.** This word can describe an extra electrical cord.

_____possession_____ **5.** This word has two sets of the same double consonants.

_____comprehension_____ **6.** This word has four syllables.

B Write the spelling words in alphabetical order.

1. _____admission_____ **2.** _____comprehension_____ **3.** _____expansion_____

4. _____extension_____ **5.** _____mission_____ **6.** _____permission_____

7. _____possession_____ **8.** _____tension_____

C Circle the word that is the same as the top one.

expansion	tension	mission	possession	comprehension
expamsion	tensiom	nission	(possession)	comprehensiom
exgansion	temsion	mision	posession	conprehension
(expansion)	(tension)	(mission)	possessiom	comperhension
expansoin	tensoin	missiom	possessoin	(comprehension)

Name _____

Lesson 25

DAY 4

Words with *-sion*

| expansion | mission | extension | possession |
| permission | tension | admission | comprehension |

A **Use the correct spelling words to complete the story.**

Our town is growing fast. Most of the _____expansion_____ is north of

town. Companies have asked for _____permission_____ from the city to

build offices there. This has caused a lot of _____tension_____ between

those who live in the north part of town and the companies. Homeowners

don't want more buildings. And they don't want more traffic near their homes.

So they've asked the city to take _____possession_____ of much of the

land. They want to have a park built so growth won't get out of control.

B **Complete each sentence with spelling words.**

1. "Comprehend" is the root word of _____comprehension_____ .

2. "Expand" is the root word of _____expansion_____ .

3. "Permit" is the root word of _____permission_____ .

4. "Admit" is the root word of _____admission_____ .

5. _____Tension_____ and _____mission_____ are two-syllable words.

C **Use each spelling word in a sentence.**

admission _____

tension _____

mission _____

extension _____

possession _____

threw	caution	education	vision	confusion
through	direction	transportation	invasion	television
patience	operation	construction	decision	explosion
patients	affection	protection	erosion	collision

A   **Write a spelling word under each picture.**

1. _____affection_____
2. _____collision_____
3. _____television_____

B   **Fill in each blank with a spelling word.**

1. Which _____direction_____ is the wind blowing?

2. It is important to study and get a good _____education_____ .

3. Please walk up the stairs and _____through_____ those doors.

4. His grandfather taught him _____patience_____ and kindness.

5. She bought a new pair of glasses to correct her _____vision_____ .

6. The cabin provided _____protection_____ from the snowstorm.

7. My little sister sometimes throws _____caution_____ to the wind.

8. They are planning the _____construction_____ of the new school.

9. The doctor has to take care of many _____patients_____ .

10. She _____threw_____ the football across the field to her friend.

11. He made the _____decision_____ to attend the play.

12. The constant rain caused the _____erosion_____ of this soil.

Name _____

likable	believable	who's	mission	expansion
usable	returnable	whose	tension	possession
movable	breakable	your	extension	permission
lovable	valuable	you're	admission	comprehension

C **Find the missing letters. Then write the word.**

1. w __h__ __o__ s __e__   whose

2. __m__ i __s__ s __i__ __o__ n   mission

3. __c__ om __p__ r e __h__ e n s i o n   comprehension

4. __l__ i __k__ a __b__ __l__ e   likable

5. __y__ o __u__ __r__   your

6. p __e__ r __m__ i s s __i__ o n   permission

D **Use the correct spelling words to complete the story.**

I like to hear my grandmother tell stories. I can listen to her for hours.

Once she told me a remarkable but ___believable___ tale that happened

during the Great Depression. Most people at that time were poor and had little to

eat. One day someone came to my grandmother's door and asked for something

to eat. Food was very ___valuable___ at that time, but she decided to give

him some. She gave him soup in a ___breakable___ dish. The dish was so

hot that he dropped it! Of course, the dish was no longer ___usable___.

But he promised to work to repay her for her kindness. My grandmother was

so impressed with what he had done that she asked him to stay. One year later

she married him!

Homonyms

| coarse | idol | vain | flee |
| course | idle | vein | flea |

A Fill in each blank with a spelling word.

1. We tried in _____vain_____ to get tickets to the concert.

2. Of _____course_____ we will go to the soccer game.

3. The vest was made of _____coarse_____ fabric.

4. I hope that wasn't a _____flea_____ on my dog.

5. His _____idol_____ is Martin Luther King, Jr.

6. I'd like to go to the beach and be _____idle_____ for a while.

7. The animals were able to _____flee_____ from the wildfire.

8. Do you know the difference between a _____vein_____ and an artery?

B Fill in the boxes with the correct spelling words.

1. | i | d | o | l |

2. | v | e | i | n |

3. | c | o | u | r | s | e |

4. | v | a | i | n |

5. | i | d | l | e |

6. | c | o | a | r | s | e |

7. | f | l | e | e |

8. | f | l | e | a |

C Complete each sentence.

1. My <u>idol</u> is _____ because _____.

2. The <u>coarse</u> _____.

Name _____

Homonyms

coarse	idol	vain	flee
course	idle	vein	flea

A Find the missing letters. Then write the word.

1. __f__ __l__ __e__ a   flea

2. __i__ __d__ l __e__   idle

3. __v__ a __i__ __n__   vain

4. __c__ __o__ u __r__ __s__ __e__   course

B Write the correct spelling word beside each clue.

_____vein_____ **1.** blood vessel

_____idle_____ **2.** inactive

_____flea_____ **3.** insect

_____course_____ **4.** route

_____flee_____ **5.** run away

_____coarse_____ **6.** rough

_____idol_____ **7.** one that is adored

_____vain_____ **8.** very proud

C Circle the word that is the same as the top one.

coarse	course	idol	idle	vein	vain
coanse	cuorse	ibol	idel	veim	voin
coares	coures	idal	ible	vien	(vain)
(coarse)	(course)	(idol)	(idle)	(vein)	vian
caorse	conrse	idot	idlc	wein	vaim

Homonyms

coarse	idol	vain	flee
course	idle	vein	flea

A Use the correct spelling words to complete the story.

My dog Boy is eleven years old. He doesn't run around as often as he used

to. The ____coarse____ hair around his muzzle is turning gray.

Cats used to ____flee____ when he was outside. Now they fearlessly

walk through our yard, while he sits ____idle____ on the front porch. Not

even a pesky ____flea____ bothers him anymore.

I'll always love old Boy. And he's still my best friend.

B Fill in each blank with the correct word.

1. "Vain" and ____vein____ are homonyms.

2. "Flee" and ____flea____ are pronounced the same.

3. ____Idle____ and ____idol____ have two syllables.

4. "Coarse" and ____course____ are pronounced the same.

5. "Coarse" and "course" are ____homonyms____ .

6. A ____homonym____ for "idle" is ____idol____ .

7. "Vein" and ____vain____ are ____homonyms____ .

C Write the spelling words in alphabetical order.

1. ____coarse____   2. ____course____   3. ____flea____

4. ____flee____   5. ____idle____   6. ____idol____

7. ____vain____   8. ____vein____

Name _____

Lesson 26 Homonyms

DAY 4

coarse	idol	vain	flee
course	idle	vein	flea

A Use each spelling word in a sentence.

course _____

idle _____

flee _____

vain _____

B Put an *X* on the word that is <u>not</u> the same.

1. coarse	coarse	coarse	co~~u~~rse	coarse
2. vain	va~~n~~e	vain	vain	vain
3. course	course	course	course	cou~~r~~ce
4. idol	idol	id~~o~~l	idol	idol

C Complete each phrase with a spelling word.

1. ___coarse___ cloth

2. to ___flee___ the country

3. a teenage ___idol___

4. a ___flea___ collar

5. ___idle___ time

6. a ___vein___ in the arm

7. a ___vain___ attempt

8. an obstacle ___course___

9. ___coarse___ manners

DAY 1

Words with *-ence*

confidence	violence	conference	independence
experience	difference	coincidence	competence

A Fill in each blank with a spelling word.

1. We met in New Orleans by _____coincidence_____.

2. Many people believe there's too much _____violence_____ on TV.

3. Her _____confidence_____ in herself helped her get the job.

4. Winning a gold medal is an _____experience_____ she'll never forget.

5. The United States declared its _____independence_____ from England in 1776.

6. I attended a _____conference_____ on writing for magazines.

7. What's the _____difference_____ between butter and margarine?

8. The committee questioned his _____competence_____ to do the job.

B Put an *X* on the word that is <u>not</u> the same.

1. confidence	confidence	confi~~d~~emce	confidence
2. experience	experience	experience	expe~~r~~eince
3. violence	voil~~e~~nce	violence	violence
4. competence	competence	con~~p~~etence	competence
5. independence	independence	independence	indepe~~n~~bence

C Write the spelling words in alphabetical order.

1. ____coincidence____ 2. ____competence____ 3. ____conference____

4. ____confidence____ 5. ____difference____ 6. ____experience____

7. ____independence____ 8. ____violence____

Name _____

117

Words with -ence

confidence	violence	conference	independence
experience	difference	coincidence	competence

A Find the missing letters. Then write the word.

1. v i o l e n c e   ___violence___

2. e x p e r i e n c e   ___experience___

3. d i f f e r e n c e   ___difference___

4. c o i n c i d e n c e   ___coincidence___

B Write the correct spelling word beside each clue.

___competence___ **1.** the state of being competent

___independence___ **2.** the opposite of dependence

___conference___ **3.** a meeting for discussion

___confidence___ **4.** feeling certain

___coincidence___ **5.** two things that happen at the same time by accident

___difference___ **6.** the state of being different

___violence___ **7.** brutal action

C Complete each sentence with spelling words.

1. The three words with four syllables are ___experience___, ___independence___, and ___coincidence___.

2. ___Difference___ has a double consonant.

3. The first four letters of these words are the same: ___confidence___ and ___conference___.

DAY 3

Words with -*ence*

confidence   violence   conference   independence

experience   difference   coincidence   competence

A **Find each hidden word from the list.**

confidence   independence   consequence

experience   difference   competence

violence   conference   coincidence

```
d  c  o  i  n  c  i  d  e  n  c  e  p  i  d
c  o  m  p  e  t  e  n  c  e  x  x  d  n  o
i  n  d  e  p  e  n  d  e  n  c  e  i  d  n
e  s  c  o  i  n  c  i  d  e  n  c  f  e  f
x  e  x  p  e  r  i  e  n  c  e  e  f  p  a
p  q  c  o  n  v  i  o  l  e  n  c  e  e  r
e  u  i  n  d  e  p  e  n  d  e  n  r  c  e
r  e  e  c  o  n  f  i  d  e  n  c  e  d  n
i  n  c  o  n  f  e  r  e  n  c  e  n  n  e
e  c  o  n  s  e  q  u  e  n  c  e  c  n  e
n  k  c  e  c  o  m  p  e  t  e  n  e  c  t
```

B **Write the root word of each spelling word.**

1. confidence ___confide___   2. competence ___compete___

3. conference ___confer___   4. difference ___differ___

C **Fill in each blank.**

1. Each spelling word ends with the letters ___ence___.

2. Which spelling words can stand alone without the ending "ence"?

___difference___   ___conference___

Name _____

Words with -ence

confidence	violence	conference	independence
experience	difference	coincidence	competence

A **Use the correct spelling words to complete the story.**

Some students get summer jobs to earn extra money. From this

_____experience_____, there's much they can learn. They may bag

groceries, cook food, or cut people's grass. Doing their jobs well will give

them greater _____confidence_____. They'll learn to take pride in their

work. Being responsible for doing a job is a big step toward

_____independence_____.

B **Complete each sentence.**

1. I have the most <u>confidence</u> when I _____

_____.

2. When I see <u>violence</u>, _____.

3. Our <u>conference</u> was _____.

4. Independence is _____

_____.

5. My <u>experience</u> taught me _____

_____.

6. My greatest <u>competence</u> is _____.

7. The <u>difference</u> between _____

_____.

8. It was a <u>coincidence</u> that _____

_____.

Lesson 28

Words with -ance

| attendance | finance | endurance | appearance |
| admittance | entrance | ambulance | performance |

A **Fill in each blank with a spelling word.**

1. Our chorus gave a great _____performance_____ last night.

2. _____Attendance_____ at the football game reached a record high.

3. The _____entrance_____ to the garden was filled with lovely plants.

4. A marathon is a test of _____endurance_____.

5. The sign on the door said "No _____admittance_____."

6. The _____ambulance_____ arrived at the scene of the accident.

7. A person's _____appearance_____ is very important when interviewing for a job.

8. The secretary of _____finance_____ manages the money.

B **Fill in the boxes with the correct spelling words.**

1.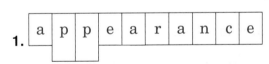

2.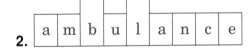

3.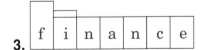

4.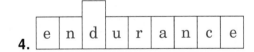

5.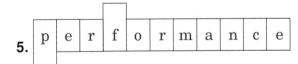

6.

7.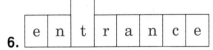

8.

C **How many spelling words begin with vowels?** _____six_____

Name _____

121

Words with -*ance*

attendance	finance	endurance	appearance
admittance	entrance	ambulance	performance

A Write the root word of each spelling word.

1. attendance _____attend_____ **2.** entrance _____enter_____

3. admittance _____admit_____ **4.** endurance _____endure_____

5. performance _____perform_____ **6.** appearance _____appear_____

B Put an *X* on the word that is <u>not</u> the same.

1. ambulance	ambulance	anb~~u~~ance	ambulance
2. performance	performance	performance	prefo~~r~~mance
3. entrance	enta~~r~~nce	entrance	entrance

C Write the correct spelling word beside each clue.

_____finance_____ **1.** money matters

_____endurance_____ **2.** the power to withstand hardship

_____ambulance_____ **3.** a vehicle for taking people to the hospital

_____appearance_____ **4.** something that appears

_____attendance_____ **5.** the act of attending

_____performance_____ **6.** a play or concert

_____admittance_____ **7.** permission to enter

_____entrance_____ **8.** the opposite of exit

D Write the spelling words that have double consonants.

_____attendance_____   _____admittance_____   _____appearance_____

Words with *-ance*

attendance	finance	endurance	appearance
admittance	entrance	ambulance	performance

A Find the missing letters. Then write the word.

1. p e r f o r m a n c e   performance

2. f i n a n c e   finance

3. a m b u l a n c e   ambulance

4. a t t e n d a n c e   attendance

B Circle the word that is the same as the top one.

admittance	endurance	entrance	appearance	performance
(admittance)	endunance	entramce	appeanance	perfromance
abmittance	enburance	(entrance)	appaerance	pertormance
admitance	enduranec	enlrance	apearance	(performance)
admittamce	(endurance)	entnarce	(appearance)	performamce

C Fill in each blank with a spelling word.

entrance — 1. If you take away the first two letters, the remaining word means "a dazed state."

appearance — 2. This word has the name of a fruit in it.

attendance — 3. This word has a number in it.

admittance — 4. This word has the name of something worn by baseball catchers.

finance — 5. If you rearrange the letters in this word, you get the words "can" and "fine."

performance — 6. The words "for man" are in this word.

Name _____

123

Lesson 28

DAY 4

Words with -ance

attendance	finance	endurance	appearance
admittance	entrance	ambulance	performance

A Write the spelling words in alphabetical order.

1. admittance
2. ambulance
3. appearance
4. attendance
5. endurance
6. entrance
7. finance
8. performance

B Use the correct spelling words to complete the story.

Last night, I saw a __performance__ of one of my favorite rock bands. To gain __admittance__ to the concert, I had to have a special badge. I received the badge when I bought my ticket.

The band made its __appearance__ on the stage at nine o'clock. They sounded great. Over ten thousand fans were in __attendance__. It was a night I'll never forget.

C Below are guide words. Write the spelling word that would come between each pair in the dictionary.

__attendance__ **1.** appoint—attic

__ambulance__ **2.** advice—annual

__endurance__ **3.** enter—enhance

__finance__ **4.** exit—future

D Write the shortest and the longest spelling words.

__finance__   __performance__

DAY
1

Words with -*y*

company	mystery	library	country
factory	apology	enemy	biology

A **Fill in each blank with a spelling word.**

1. The equipment is assembled at the _____factory_____ .

2. _____Biology_____ is the study of life.

3. I hope you'll accept my _____apology_____ .

4. We expected our _____company_____ to arrive about 6 o'clock.

5. Our _____library_____ has some interesting books about animals.

6. The _____mystery_____ of the missing diamond has never been solved.

7. The hawk is an _____enemy_____ of the mouse.

8. We've traveled outside our own _____country_____ many times.

B **Find the missing letters. Then write the word.**

1. c _o_ m _p_ _a_ _n_ y   _____company_____

2. _a_ p _o_ l _o_ g _y_   _____apology_____

3. _f_ a c t _o_ r _y_   _____factory_____

C **Complete each sentence with spelling words.**

1. _____Library_____ and _____biology_____ have a long *i* sound.

2. _____Apology_____ and _____enemy_____ begin with vowels.

3. The word with the fewest number of syllables is _____country_____ .

4. The two words that rhyme are _____apology_____ and _____biology_____ .

5. The two words beginning with the same letter are _____company_____ and _____country_____ .

Name _____

DAY
2

Words with -*y*

| company | mystery | library | country |
| factory | apology | enemy | biology |

A Put an *X* on the word that is <u>not</u> the same.

1. company	company	company	con~~p~~any	company
2. factory	fac~~t~~ony	factory	factory	factory
3. mystery	mystery	mys~~t~~rey	mystery	mystery
4. apology	apology	apology	apology	apo~~l~~ogy
5. library	lid~~r~~ary	library	library	library
6. enemy	enemy	enemy	em~~e~~my	enemy
7. country	country	con~~u~~try	country	country
8. biology	biology	biology	dio~~l~~ogy	biology

B Use each spelling word in a sentence.

factory _____

mystery _____

country _____

library _____

C Fill in each blank with a spelling word.

apology
_____   **1.** The word "log" is found in these two words.
biology
_____

mystery
_____   **2.** The word "my" is found in these two words.
enemy
_____

country
_____   **3.** The word "try" is found in this word.

Lesson 29

DAY 3

Words with -*y*

company	mystery	library	country
factory	apology	enemy	biology

A **Use the correct spelling words to complete the story.**

My friends and I visited a small ____company____ that makes stuffed animals. They make bears, dogs, monkeys, and rabbits. We went to the ____factory____ to watch them piece together the parts of each animal.

We asked the people at the factory how they keep track of which parts go where. They told us it's no ____mystery____. They work on the same animals on the same day. That way there's no chance of putting a bear's head on a dog's body. We learned a lot at the factory that day.

B **Which spelling word might be used in discussing each topic?**

____library____   **1.** overdue books

____enemy____   **2.** an opponent in war

____company____   **3.** guests in the home

____apology____   **4.** wrongdoing

____country____   **5.** patriotism

____biology____   **6.** studying plants and animals

____factory____   **7.** a manufacturing plant

____mystery____   **8.** something unexplained

C **Write the spelling words that have four syllables.**

____biology____   ____apology____

Name _____

Words with -*y*

| company | mystery | library | country |
| factory | apology | enemy | biology |

A Find each hidden word from the list.

company	country	county	berry
factory	biology	lady	gypsy
mystery	geometry	story	ruby
apology	chimney	pulley	army
library	journey	valley	ferry
enemy	diary	dairy	sentry

```
h  r  o  u  v  n  c  r  s  x  e  i  m  s  u
s  e  n  t  g  e  o  m  e  t  r  y  a  c  c
e  n  e  m  y  j  o  d  a  i  r  y  e  b  o
n  e  v  a  p  o  l  o  g  y  m  y  s  e  m
t  h  e  o  s  u  c  h  i  m  n  e  t  r  p
r  l  a  d  y  r  f  o  d  e  f  v  s  r  a
y  c  h  i  m  n  e  y  h  d  c  a  t  y  n
o  m  y  s  t  e  r  y  b  i  o  l  o  g  y
p  u  l  l  e  y  r  e  n  a  u  l  r  o  r
f  a  c  t  o  r  y  h  i  r  n  e  y  j  u
e  n  e  c  o  u  n  t  r  y  t  y  k  l  b
b  i  o  l  l  i  b  r  a  r  y  a  r  m  y
g  s  m  o  y  l  e  f  r  s  m  x  d  c  h
```

B Write the spelling words in alphabetical order.

1. _____apology_____   2. _____biology_____   3. _____company_____

4. _____country_____   5. _____enemy_____   6. _____factory_____

7. _____library_____   8. _____mystery_____

Lesson 30 Homonyms

DAY 1

principal	guest	aloud	presence
principle	guessed	allowed	presents

A Fill in each blank with a spelling word.

1. He was admired as a man of ___principle___ .

2. No one was ___allowed___ to swim in the lake before the month of May.

3. I ___guessed___ it would take five hours to drive to the beach.

4. Her favorite ___presents___ were the wristwatch and the trip to the city on the train.

5. She recited the poem ___aloud___ to herself.

6. I was a ___guest___ at their house for three days.

7. The ___principal___ of our school is very nice.

8. Her ___presence___ was felt in the room.

B Fill in the boxes with the correct spelling words.

1. p r e s e n c e

2. g u e s t

3. p r i n c i p a l

4. g u e s s e d

5. p r i n c i p l e

6. p r e s e n t s

7. a l o u d

8. a l l o w e d

Name _____

Homonyms

principal	guest	aloud	presence
principle	guessed	allowed	presents

A Write a spelling word under each picture.

1. ___principal___   2. ___guest___   3. ___presents___

B Write the correct spelling word beside each clue.

___aloud___   **1.** louder than a whisper

___guest___   **2.** visitor

___principle___   **3.** a basic truth or law

___presence___   **4.** the condition of being present

___presents___   **5.** gifts

___principal___   **6.** a person with authority

___guessed___   **7.** supposed without much information

___allowed___   **8.** permitted

C Write the spelling words in alphabetical order.

1. ___allowed___   2. ___aloud___   3. ___guessed___

4. ___guest___   5. ___presence___   6. ___presents___

7. ___principal___   8. ___principle___

D Write the spelling words that have three syllables.

___principal___   ___principle___

DAY 3

Homonyms

principal	guest	aloud	presence
principle	guessed	allowed	presents

A Find the missing letters. Then write the word.

1. g u e s s e d   _____guessed_____

2. p r i n c i p l e   _____principle_____

3. p r e s e n c e   _____presence_____

4. a l l o w e d   _____allowed_____

B Below are guide words. Write the spelling word that would come between each pair in the dictionary.

_____aloud_____ **1.** alone—alphabet

_____guessed_____ **2.** gone—guessing

_____presence_____ **3.** prepare—presented

_____principal_____ **4.** prime—principals

C Fill in each blank with a spelling word.

1. _____Presents_____ is a plural word.

2. The words with double consonants are _____allowed_____ and _____guessed_____.

3. The words that can mean a person are _____principal_____ and _____guest_____.

4. Write the words that come from these root words.

guess _____guessed_____   allow _____allowed_____

present _____presents_____

Name _____

 # Homonyms

principal	guest	aloud	presence
principle	guessed	allowed	presents

A **Use each spelling word in a sentence.**

principal _____

aloud _____

allowed _____

presence _____

guest _____

B **Circle the word that is the same as the top one.**

principle	guessed	allowed	presents	presence
prinicple	guesseb	allawed	presemts	presents
prinicipal	geussed	(allowed)	persents	presemce
pirnciple	(guessed)	alouwed	(presents)	presnece
primciple	quessed	alloued	presnets	(presence)
(principle)	guesesd	alloweb	bresents	persence

C **Use the correct spelling words to complete the story.**

You've reached the end of this book. By now you know that the main

_____principle_____ of good spelling is to practice each day.

Could you have _____guessed_____, many weeks ago, that you would

know how to spell so many words? Learning to spell correctly and to write

well are like _____presents_____ that no one else can give you. You give

them to yourself by working hard and always using what you've learned.

attendance	finance	flee	company	library
admittance	entrance	flea	factory	enemy
endurance	appearance	vain	mystery	guest
ambulance	performance	vein	apology	principal

A **Write a spelling word under each picture.**

1. _____ambulance_____ 2. _____guest_____ 3. _____principal_____

B **Fill in each blank with a spelling word.**

1. I offered an _____apology_____ to her because I was wrong.

2. The large _____attendance_____ at the theater on opening night was more

   than we expected.

3. We searched in _____vain_____ for our lost cat.

4. I enjoy the _____company_____ of good friends.

5. Does your uncle work at that _____factory_____?

6. What is in outer space is a _____mystery_____ to many people.

7. It takes _____endurance_____ to work twelve hours a day.

8. The singer will make an _____appearance_____ on Saturday night.

9. Her _____performance_____ at the show was the best I had ever seen.

10. The forest fire caused the animals to _____flee_____.

11. I need to return these books to the public _____library_____.

Name _____

violence	experience	idol	biology	country
conference	difference	idle	principle	guessed
competence	coincidence	coarse	presents	aloud
confidence	independence	course	presence	allowed

C **Find the missing letters. Then write the word.**

1. __b__ i __o__ l __o__ __g__ __y__   biology

2. __g__ u e __s__ __s__ __e__ d   guessed

3. __c__ o u __r__ __s__ e   course

4. __d__ i f __f__ e r __e__ __n__ c e   difference

5. p __r__ __e__ s e __n__ c e   presence

6. i n d __e__ __p__ e n __d__ e n c e   independence

D **Use the correct spelling words to complete the story.**

My cousin is trying out a new career. He wants to be a teacher. Though he

lacks ____experience____ in this new field, he has ____confidence____ in himself.

He believes he will gain ____competence____ and succeed.

His guiding ____principle____ has always been "never say never." He

repeats this and several other sayings ____aloud____ to himself every day.

It may be a ____coincidence____, but he has always been very successful in

everything he does. He has many friends, and most people like to be in his

____presence____. I think he will make a great teacher!

My Word List

Words I Can Spell

Put a ✓ in the box beside each word you spell correctly on your weekly test.

1

☐ unaware   ☐ unsafe

☐ unhealthy   ☐ unhappy

☐ unequal   ☐ unjust

☐ unlikely   ☐ uncertain

2

☐ nonstop   ☐ nonfat

☐ nonsense   ☐ nonliving

☐ nonsmoking   ☐ nonfiction

☐ nonstick   ☐ nonbreakable

3

☐ preview   ☐ preschool

☐ precook   ☐ preheat

☐ pretest   ☐ prepaid

☐ prepare   ☐ prevent

4

☐ peace   ☐ bow

☐ piece   ☐ bough

☐ some   ☐ waist

☐ sum   ☐ waste

5

☐ dislike   ☐ discount

☐ disappear   ☐ disconnect

☐ disagree   ☐ disinfect

☐ dishonest   ☐ disorganize

Words To Review

If you miss a word on your test, write it here. Practice it until you can spell it correctly. Then check the box beside the word.

_____

_____

_____

_____

_____

_____

_____

_____

_____

_____

_____

_____

_____

_____

_____

_____

_____

_____

_____

_____

Name _____

135

My Word List

Words I Can Spell

Put a ✓ in the box beside each word you spell correctly on your weekly test.

6

- [ ] subway
- [ ] subzero
- [ ] subfreezing
- [ ] suburban
- [ ] submarine
- [ ] subtitle
- [ ] subsoil
- [ ] submerge

7

- [ ] refill
- [ ] recycle
- [ ] review
- [ ] refund
- [ ] repair
- [ ] recharge
- [ ] reclaim
- [ ] rewind

8

- [ ] rain
- [ ] rein
- [ ] their
- [ ] there
- [ ] haul
- [ ] hall
- [ ] pair
- [ ] pear

9

- [ ] misplace
- [ ] misprint
- [ ] mislead
- [ ] misbehave
- [ ] mistreat
- [ ] misuse
- [ ] misfortune
- [ ] misunderstand

10

- [ ] contract
- [ ] concert
- [ ] congregate
- [ ] concern
- [ ] conform
- [ ] confide
- [ ] consent
- [ ] conduct

Words To Review

If you miss a word on your test, write it here. Practice it until you can spell it correctly. Then check the box beside the word.

_____

_____

_____

_____

_____

_____

_____

_____

_____

_____

_____

_____

_____

_____

_____

_____

Words I Can Spell

Put a ✓ in the box beside each word you spell correctly on your weekly test.

Words To Review

If you miss a word on your test, write it here. Practice it until you can spell it correctly. Then check the box beside the word.

11

- ☐ descend
- ☐ dehydrate
- ☐ deposit
- ☐ decide
- ☐ decrease
- ☐ deflate
- ☐ depart
- ☐ deliver

12

- ☐ throne
- ☐ thrown
- ☐ shone
- ☐ shown
- ☐ fair
- ☐ fare
- ☐ it's
- ☐ its

13

- ☐ harmless
- ☐ painless
- ☐ careless
- ☐ hopeless
- ☐ useless
- ☐ helpless
- ☐ thankless
- ☐ thoughtless

14

- ☐ thoughtful
- ☐ peaceful
- ☐ beautiful
- ☐ harmful
- ☐ careful
- ☐ truthful
- ☐ hopeful
- ☐ thankful

15

- ☐ slowness
- ☐ sickness
- ☐ coldness
- ☐ darkness
- ☐ fairness
- ☐ kindness
- ☐ blackness
- ☐ loudness

Name _____

Words I Can Spell

Put a ✓ in the box beside each word you spell correctly on your weekly test.

16

- ☐ plain
- ☐ plane
- ☐ past
- ☐ passed
- ☐ forth
- ☐ fourth
- ☐ stake
- ☐ steak

17

- ☐ friendly
- ☐ honestly
- ☐ correctly
- ☐ partly
- ☐ quickly
- ☐ quietly
- ☐ safely
- ☐ bravely

18

- ☐ statement
- ☐ argument
- ☐ equipment
- ☐ payment
- ☐ enjoyment
- ☐ retirement
- ☐ encouragement
- ☐ advertisement

19

- ☐ doe
- ☐ dough
- ☐ peer
- ☐ pier
- ☐ air
- ☐ heir
- ☐ bass
- ☐ base

20

- ☐ possible
- ☐ horrible
- ☐ edible
- ☐ audible
- ☐ terrible
- ☐ incredible
- ☐ visible
- ☐ sensible

Words To Review

If you miss a word on your test, write it here. Practice it until you can spell it correctly. Then check the box beside the word.

_____

_____

_____

_____

_____

_____

_____

_____

_____

_____

_____

_____

_____

_____

Words I Can Spell

Put a ✓ in the box beside each word you spell correctly on your weekly test.

Words To Review

If you miss a word on your test, write it here. Practice it until you can spell it correctly. Then check the box beside the word.

21

- ☐ likable
- ☐ believable
- ☐ usable
- ☐ returnable
- ☐ movable
- ☐ valuable
- ☐ lovable
- ☐ breakable

22

- ☐ patience
- ☐ patients
- ☐ threw
- ☐ through
- ☐ who's
- ☐ whose
- ☐ your
- ☐ you're

23

- ☐ caution
- ☐ direction
- ☐ education
- ☐ protection
- ☐ affection
- ☐ operation
- ☐ transportation
- ☐ construction

24

- ☐ invasion
- ☐ confusion
- ☐ decision
- ☐ television
- ☐ vision
- ☐ explosion
- ☐ erosion
- ☐ collision

25

- ☐ expansion
- ☐ permission
- ☐ mission
- ☐ tension
- ☐ extension
- ☐ admission
- ☐ possession
- ☐ comprehension

_____

_____

_____

_____

_____

_____

_____

_____

_____

_____

_____

_____

_____

_____

_____

_____

_____

_____

Name _____

Words I Can Spell

Put a ✓ in the box beside each word you spell correctly on your weekly test.

26

- ☐ coarse
- ☐ course
- ☐ idol
- ☐ idle
- ☐ vain
- ☐ vein
- ☐ flee
- ☐ flea

27

- ☐ confidence
- ☐ experience
- ☐ violence
- ☐ difference
- ☐ conference
- ☐ coincidence
- ☐ independence
- ☐ competence

28

- ☐ attendance
- ☐ admittance
- ☐ finance
- ☐ entrance
- ☐ endurance
- ☐ ambulance
- ☐ appearance
- ☐ performance

29

- ☐ company
- ☐ factory
- ☐ mystery
- ☐ apology
- ☐ library
- ☐ enemy
- ☐ country
- ☐ biology

30

- ☐ principal
- ☐ principle
- ☐ guest
- ☐ guessed
- ☐ aloud
- ☐ allowed
- ☐ presence
- ☐ presents

Words To Review

If you miss a word on your test, write it here. Practice it until you can spell it correctly. Then check the box beside the word.

Word Study Sheet

(Make a check mark after each step.)

Words	1 Look at the Word	2 Say the Word	3 Think About Each Letter	4 Spell the Word Aloud	5 Write the Word	6 Check the Spelling	7 Repeat Steps (if needed)

Name _____

141

Graph Your Progress

(Color or shade in the boxes.)

Number of words correctly spelled:

	Lesson 1	Lesson 2	Lesson 3	Lesson 4	Lesson 5	Lesson 6	Lesson 7	Lesson 8	Lesson 9	Lesson 10	Lesson 11	Lesson 12	Lesson 13	Lesson 14	Lesson 15	Lesson 16	Lesson 17	Lesson 18	Lesson 19	Lesson 20	Lesson 21	Lesson 22	Lesson 23	Lesson 24	Lesson 25	Lesson 26	Lesson 27	Lesson 28	Lesson 29	Lesson 30
8																														
7																														
6																														
5																														
4																														
3																														
2																														
1																														

142

Name _____